Your Own Worst Enemy

ALSO BY STEVEN BERGLAS

The Success Syndrome: Hitting Bottom When You Reach the Top (1986)

Self-Handicapping: The Paradox That Isn't (with R. L. Higgins and C. R. Snyder, 1990)

ALSO BY ROY F. BAUMEISTER

Identity: Cultural Change and the Struggle for Self (1986)

Public Self and Private Self (ed., 1986)

Masochism and the Self (1989)

Meanings of Life (1991)

Escaping the Self (1991)

Your Own Worst Enemy

Understanding the Paradox of Self-Defeating Behavior

STEVEN BERGLAS, PH.D.
AND
ROY F. BAUMEISTER, PH.D.

BasicBooks
A Division of HarperCollins*Publishers*

Library of Congress Cataloging-in-Publication Data
Berglas, Steven.
    Your own worst enemy : understanding the paradox of self-
defeating behavior / Steven Berglas, Roy F. Baumeister.
        p.   cm.
    Includes bibliographical references and index.
    ISBN 0–465–07680–7
    1. Self-defeating behavior. I. Baumeister, Roy F. II. Title.
RC455.4.S43B47 1993
616.85′82—dc20   92–53238
                                                                        CIP

Designed by Ellen Levine

93 94 95 96 CC/HC 9 8 7 6 5 4 3 2 1

Contents

1

Snatching Defeat from the Jaws of Victory

We has met the enemy, and it is us.
—Pogo, the cartoon character by Walt Kelly

EUGENE FODOR was the first American to win the top prize in the prestigious Tchaikovsky violin competition in Moscow. When the twenty-four-year-old violinist returned home after his victory in 1974, he received a hero's welcome, comparable to that of the young world-class pianist Van Cliburn at his peak. Fodor was given the key to New York City, invited to perform at the White House, featured frequently with Johnny Carson on the "Tonight Show," and profiled in a Dewar's Scotch advertisement. He became a media star, the Mick Jagger of classical music. Yet in the wake of his success, Fodor began struggling with a psychological demon. He alienated prospective sponsors and found his credibility with colleagues damaged as he failed to live up to expectations. He began experimenting with drugs, and when he was arrested for breaking into a hotel room at age thirty-nine, 24 grams of cocaine as well as a hypodermic needle with traces of heroin were found in his possession. His run-in with the law, reported on the front page of the *New York Times,* brought him more attention than he had received in almost ten years.[1]

People like Eugene Fodor have long perplexed philoso-
phers, theologians, mental health professionals, and anyone
else who has attempted to grasp the essence of human nature.
It is not drug use itself that is baffling; people become addicted
for countless reasons: career pressures, peer influence, a marriage gone bad, even genetic vulnerability, to name a few. The
inherently troubling aspect of the Eugene Fodors of the world
is that they turn against themselves when ostensibly they have
everything to live for. When people with the potential to enjoy
the good life instead destroy or abuse the achievements and
recognition they have worked to attain, they force us to confront a fundamental human paradox: self-defeating behavior.

If Fodor's turning against himself is hard to explain, what
are we to make of the famous French chessplayer Deschapelles? Claiming to have mastered the game of chess in two
days, he went on to succeed his teacher as champion of his
region. The time came, however, when he was no longer certain of defeating all challengers. At that point he adopted a new
condition for all matches: He would play only if his opponent
would accept the advantage of "pawn and move," removing
one of Deschapelles's pawns and making the first move, which
increased the odds that Deschapelles would lose. This strategy
became known as the *Deschapelles coup.*[2] Why would he have
insisted on terms that put him at a competitive disadvantage
and made it likely that he would lose many games?

Actually, Deschapelles showed a certain elegance in forcing
an advantage on his opponents. If he lost a game, his poor
performance would not be held to reflect a simple lack of
competence; he could point to the disadvantage as the source
of failure. Moreover, if in spite of the disadvantage he won the
game, judgments of his inherent competence would soar: My
goodness, he did that well despite a handicap?

Yet even if we assume that Deschapelles was a crafty social

strategist, a question remains: What motivated him to increase the risk of failure in order to preempt the attribution of failure? Similarly, why would Fodor throw away his success just when he had everything going for him? Different though their cases are, certain similarities emerge. Both reached the pinnacle of their professions before beginning to behave in a manner that would jeopardize their positions in their respective fields. Both had careers that required them to prove their competence over and over again. And both were soloists: the entire responsibility for success or failure fell on their shoulders. Their situations sound stressful, but is stress sufficient to account for patterns of self-defeat?

This book is devoted to understanding the behaviors of people like Deschapelles and Fodor who inflict pain, suffering, and hardships on themselves for no apparent reason. As psychologists, we have long been intrigued by this paradox. Both of us were initially trained as experimental social psychologists, but one of us (Berglas) ultimately specialized in clinical psychology and has for some years been treating the psychological disorders of people who sabotage their successes, arrange for relationships to fall through, or repeatedly engage in interactions that are designed to fail. The other (Baumeister) continued in research, seeking to understand the personality variables and social forces that make normal adults engage in patterns of self-defeat. Thus, the book reflects two different perspectives on the problem. We have been able to draw on a number of clinical cases of self-defeating behavior as well as on the products of research related to it.*

---

*In this book we use secondhand accounts of the behavior of prominent people for illustrative purposes. Our intent is to help readers identify styles of self-defeat. Unless otherwise noted, we have not had personal contact with the prominent people we discuss but rather have based our accounts of their behavior on reports in reputable media outlets. On the basis of these reports, we concluded that their

In the following chapters we examine a wide range of self-defeating behaviors with an eye toward imposing order on the varied kinds of events that qualify as self-sabotage. In doing so, we consider what goals are accomplished by behaving in a self-defeating manner and what circumstances give rise to these paradoxical behaviors. And we demonstrate just how prevalent these behaviors are. A moment's thought will bring to mind many common behavior patterns that have a decidedly self-defeating tinge:

- People continue to smoke despite overwhelming evidence linking nicotine with lung cancer and heart disease.
- Bright children fail to live up to their potential in school, neglecting homework assignments and failing to study for tests they should pass with ease.
- Professional athletes, who rely on their bodies as their primary means of support, use drugs such as cocaine or steroids, despite known health risks and the potential legal consequences if their drug use is discovered.
- Men and women with ample financial resources endure verbal and even physical abuse, harassment, and loveless lives by remaining in obviously dysfunctional marriages when neither religious constraints nor the needs of children explain why they tolerate emotional pain instead of obtaining a divorce.

---

behavior *appeared representative* of recognized patterns of self-defeating behavior. Our analysis is neither intended to diagnose the behavior of any public figure nor to suggest that they are, or were once, suffering a psychological disorder.

When we report clinical case histories, the identifying features of the patient have been intentionally distorted to protect his or her anonymity—a standard practice for reporting psychotherapeutic casework. For example, data such as age, career, number and sex of children, and religious affiliation have been altered if unrelated to a patient's self-defeating character style. Data crucial to understanding an individual's self-defeating style, such as his or her marital status, have not been changed.

WHATEVER HAPPENED TO THE PLEASURE PRINCIPLE?

A collective self-conception among all peoples is that we humans are a selfish, hedonistic species. Most modern ideas about human behavior, relying heavily on Freudian theory, suggest that it is natural to seek to reduce pain. Human behavior is thought to be regulated by the so-called *pleasure principle,* a term coined by Freud[3] to account for the way humans respond to unpleasurable states (for example, tension) or feelings (for example, anger) by seeking to relieve them through behaviors designed to afford pleasure. From infants who cry in response to hunger pangs, to adults who spend countless hours (not to mention dollars) in psychotherapy attempting to resolve psychological pain, human nature seems totally opposed to enduring any displeasure.

Historically, this natural tendency to pursue pleasure has at times evoked concern that the avoidance of pain may lead people to ignore the suffering of others. Medieval theology included six acts of self-centeredness (covetousness, envy, gluttony, lust, pride, and sloth) among its seven deadly sins; and of the Ten Commandments, the cornerstone of Judeo-Christian ethics, half warn humankind against harming others en route to self-satisfaction.

Today, however, we Americans seem less troubled by the presumption that we are self-indulgent hedonists than by the threat of the opposite: the possibility that we all may have the seeds of Eugene Fodor's self-destructiveness within us. We take for granted that winning is a good thing ("the only thing," according to football coaching legend Vince Lombardi), and we revere winners. Self-help books that advocate beating the competition and becoming number one—no matter what it takes—spend months on the best-seller lists.[4] There is even a sense that our culture actively dislikes the person who will not pursue hedonistic gratification en route to the top. We are perplexed and disquieted by the paradox of the act or pattern of actions that violates the pleasure principle through self-defeat.

Self-defeat takes many forms, few as obvious as Eugene Fodor's fall from stardom. More typically, self-defeatists arrange to end up "inadvertently" or "unwittingly" in situations or relationships that cause them pain. In fact, a great many self-defeating patterns are found within the structure of marriages or other close relationships. One bizarre tale of self-destructive romance ended with a local "golden boy," scion of a family of cotton plantation owners, accused of murdering his beautiful ex-wife and pleading with police who arrested him, "Please kill me. . . . Women make you do funny things."[5] When the facts surrounding the case of Ralph Hand III were made public, the alleged murderer's remark seemed an understatement.

Ralph Hand III was both blessed and cursed: blessed with inherited wealth and cursed in having lost the use of his legs in an automobile accident during his freshman year in college. He had married Olivia, a vivacious young woman from a poor local family, who had returned to her hometown after the failures of her first marriage and a fledgling career. On their wedding day Olivia kept Ralph waiting at the altar for forty-five minutes, and things went quickly downhill from there. Their tempestuous thirteen-month marriage was said to have been marked by a chronic pattern of drunken brawls. When the paraplegic Hand was able to initiate brawls, he would use his overdeveloped arms to beat his wife severely. Yet she was often able to gain an advantage by snatching his walker from him and using it to beat him as he crawled on the floor.

In spite of what might appear to be the couple's unmitigated contempt for each other, their friends claim that even after the

Hands were divorced, they met secretly to fulfill their mutual obsessive desire. One witness told police that months before her death, a drunken Olivia had proclaimed: "Ralph is my man, and nobody will take him from me. . . . They'll have to kill me." According to police in Tallahatchie County, Mississippi, her former husband, in fact, did just that.[6]

The Hands' marriage is not unique in the annals of self-defeating behavior patterns. A far more celebrated, albeit fictitious, case of ongoing mutual abuse is chronicled in Edward Albee's play *Who's Afraid of Virginia Woolf?* The protagonists, George and Martha, raise abuse to the level of art. While obviously every bit as contemptuous of each other as the Hands, they are far too civil—some would argue sick—to divorce or end their involvement through murder. George and Martha need each other and make sure that their life mates are around to satisfy their deep-seated psychological disturbances.

Yet we must ask several questions after witnessing the brawls they endure: Precisely what could this need be? Why endure—actually, foster—a relationship that promises to inflict pain? Why do people like Ralph, Olivia, George, and Martha bypass opportunities to end their pain and continue to subject themselves to abusive mates? These are among the many perplexing questions that we address throughout this book.

Unlike the Hands or George and Martha, Charles Stuart seemed to have chosen a wonderful mate. In fact, judging from outward appearances, he seemed to be governed by the pleasure principle. Although he may not have qualified for Ralph Hand's golden-boy status, he certainly seemed to have achieved the American dream. Stuart had married a lovely, bright young woman, Carol, who in late 1989, while working as an attorney for a major publishing company, was carrying their baby. At that time Stuart was the manager of an exclusive

Boston fur salon, earning a six-figure salary. He dressed well, owned an expensive suburban home, and could afford the luxury of a car phone. Anyone who knew what Charles Stuart had would wonder how someone could want for more. Yet apparently he did.

On October 23, 1989, residents of the greater metropolitan Boston area, and soon thereafter of the entire nation, were shocked to learn that as Charles Stuart and his wife were driving home from a birthing class, they took a wrong turn, entered a mostly black neighborhood, and allegedly were attacked by a gun-wielding black man. Carol Stuart died within hours from a gunshot wound to her head; her child, delivered by emergency surgery, died days later. Charles Stuart, critically wounded from a gunshot wound to his lower abdomen, would ultimately recover to receive a wave of sympathy from around the United States. He was instantly judged to be the quintessential innocent victim—and would have remained so, but all evidence gathered after the incident pointed to Charles Stuart as both victim and perpetrator. Like Eugene Fodor, he had turned against himself when he appeared to be on top of the world.

Charles Stuart leaped from a bridge to his death on January 4, 1990, following weeks of news reports suggesting that he may have been involved in the murder of his pregnant wife and unborn child. It is not entirely certain that Stuart actually fired the gunshots that killed his wife and maimed him; he may have had an accomplice pull the trigger. What *is* certain is that he both orchestrated the shooting and engaged in an elaborate coverup scheme. He disposed of his wife's valuables to make the motive for the attack appear to be black poverty attacking white affluence. And he caused himself severe bodily trauma during the staged crime, risking a lifetime of pain from a near-mortal wound, for an end that defies reason.

Since Charles Stuart took his own life after suffering from what appeared to be self-destructiveness, rather than victimization, we can never determine his motivation for resorting to self-defeat. The Boston media instantly postulated that he had committed the crime for the basest of motives: sex (he was linked romantically with a "beautiful blonde," a story ultimately refuted) and money (estimates of the life insurance policies he had on his wife ranged from $100,000 to $480,000). Yet if he had wanted out of his marriage and onto a faster track in life, why would he have endured a terrible self-inflicted wound instead of simply hiring a thug to kill his wife? Somehow, someone obsessed with self-aggrandizing outcomes— money, fame, and "trophy" lovers—would not seem the type who would harm himself. Or would he?

In fact, recall the Deschapelles coup. Many self-defeating strategies involve the acquisition of a handicap, wound, burden, or disease. The struggle that self-imposed hardships create is an interesting one indeed. By externalizing the ostensible cause of their suffering and making it appear as though they are being victimized by forces outside themselves, self-defeatists attempt to convince themselves and others that an external cure for their situation can be found. All they need is a better medication, therapist, spouse, job, school, or neighborhood, they argue; then their truly healthy internal selves will emerge, and their problems will end. In the meantime, since they appear to be striving to achieve a successful and satisfying life, they are left alone to orchestrate their own demise. Something about prevailing despite hardships appeals to these people and can be an effective mechanism for maintaining self-esteem. Yet given the risks inherent in acquiring such handicaps, we must ask why people go to such great lengths to control how they appear in others' eyes.

Consider the number of actors, athletes, and writers who are hampered in their pursuit of creative success by seemingly external agents. Part of the mystique surrounding the avant-garde lifestyle is the use of mind- or mood-altering drugs to enhance creativity. Yet drugs not only impede the long-term functioning of the mind but threaten life itself. Why, then, do so many artists who claim to use drugs as agents of self-enhancement ultimately employ them to engineer their personal and professional demises?

Lenny Bruce, Freddie Prinze, and John Belushi—like so many pathetic Pagliaccis—orchestrated their own drug-induced deaths as they made others laugh. Self-destruction via substance abuse among stage and screen performers (Judy Garland, Marilyn Monroe, and Elvis Presley are but a few who come to mind) has become so commonplace that we hardly notice those luminaries (such as Jason Robards and Elizabeth Taylor) who survive battles with the bottle or pills. In the world of literature and journalism, creativity is often linked with intoxication, and such geniuses as Tennessee Williams and Truman Capote virtually drowned themselves in alcohol.

The use of drugs among talented athletes is equally commonplace and even harder to comprehend, because in using substances that impair the functioning of the body, the chemically dependent athlete is contradicting fundamental training principles that value nurturing—as opposed to stressing—the body. Yet there is a growing epidemic of athletes, from varsity ranks to the pros, who destroy themselves under the guise of using pharmacological aids to cope with the pressures of competition or seven-figure salaries. In recent years, superstars such as Derek Sanderson, Len Bias, Dwight Gooden, Darryl Strawberry, and Dexter Manley all began abusing alcohol or drugs after reaching the top of their respective fields. Instances of self-sabotage among star athletic performers have prompted organizations such as the National Collegiate Athletic Association and the National Basketball Association to establish substance-abuse prevention and treatment programs.

A comparable pattern of self-destructiveness among athletes involves the use of life- and career-threatening drugs to enhance performance. It is hard to imagine that champion sprinter Ben Johnson envisioned anything other than winning gold medals when he began using steroids in preparation for the 1988 Olympic Games in Seoul. What astounds those who followed his tragedy is that he failed to discontinue the use of these drugs in time to avoid detection by Olympic authorities. If Ben Johnson had a single-minded desire to succeed, why would he not destroy evidence of the one activity that, if detected, could potentially ensure his ultimate defeat?

The failure to conceal damaging evidence is not confined to the world of sports. Former Senator Gary Hart's affair with model Donna Rice is a glaring example. At the height of his campaign for the 1988 Democratic nomination for president, Hart held a news conference to address issues about his character and challenged reporters who doubted his marital fidelity to follow him for the remainder of the campaign. As we all know, this dare ended his political career. Within weeks of the news conference Hart was photographed with Rice, yachting off the coast of Florida, and the viability of his candidacy was over.

The commotion generated by Hart's involvement with Rice stemmed from what most observers judged to be his "self-destructiveness."[7] Extramarital affairs are not necessarily self-defeating acts. When conducted discreetly, they may arguably be healthy adaptations to irreconcilably failed marriages, or perhaps even benign indulgences of sexual cravings. Yet Hart's involvement with Rice led directly to his professional undoing. Is it safe to assume that he wanted out of his marriage?

Doubtful, since soon after their affair became public, Hart and Rice split up, and the former senator is still with his wife. Did he want out of politics? He vigorously denied that possibility in 1987, but it is the outcome he achieved. Or was there a method to Hart's "madness," hidden to the world and relevant only to his personal sense of self?

Other powerful political figures have met with a fate comparable to Hart's after cavorting with paramours in public; Wilbur Mills's drunken public displays of affection for stripper Fanny Foxx, for example, cost him his congressional seat in 1974. Such cases, like Eugene Fodor's, call into question the alleged benefits of reaching the top of one's profession. If all the secrets of the lives of the rich and famous were known, it would be clear that many such people (or those poised for wealth and fame) pursue an agent or agency capable of bringing about their downfall.

Certainly this was true of the televangelism empires that flourished during the 1980s only to implode in the early 1990s after a series of sexual indiscretions and greedy fiascoes became public. The bubble of sanctity surrounding this industry first burst when Jessica Hahn reported having been drugged and coerced into having sex with the Reverend Jim Bakker. Bakker and his PTL ministry were subsequently found to have given Hahn six-figure payoffs to remain silent about this affair, and he was later convicted of defrauding followers who had invested in real-estate projects sponsored by his ministry. A footnote to Bakker's self-inflicted demise was furnished by the Reverend Jimmy Swaggart, who was disgraced and bankrupted after prostitutes publicized his longtime involvement with them.

The sexual appetites of men like Hart, Bakker, and Swaggart would not be discussed in this book or in the national media were they not all married and, by their own choosing, prominently positioned in the public eye. Since these men professed to be guided by a high moral calling, the fact that they were found to be engaged in illicit and immoral acts left observers no choice but to infer some motive running counter to self-preservation.

Again and again, one is bewildered by the actions of a man or woman with all the observable material rewards that life has to offer acting in a manner that contradicts not only the pleasure principle, but the laws of economics as well. Consider the 1980s, when it seemed the economic boom would last forever—and when multimillionaires, like Ivan Boesky and Michael Milken, from many of our most prestigious financial institutions became involved in a series of self-destructive debacles. Wall Street's insider-trading scandal saw dozens of men with seven-figure incomes risking (and ultimately destroying) their careers for cash payoffs of less than 10 percent of their net worth. A baffled public asked, What made them do it?

Equally startling is the saga of Leona Helmsley, the billionaire real-estate baroness convicted on several counts of tax evasion, embezzlement, and extortion. Apart from the fact that her allegedly abhorrent personality incurred the wrath of the New York City press corps, the aspect of her trial that garnered the most attention was the risk-to-reward ratio of her illegal activities. Court documents revealed that the total dollar amount of her misappropriations was under $2 million—less than 1 percent of her net worth.

The preceding examples may suggest that self-defeat occurs only among the prominent, but that is far from the case. Although instances of self-defeat among the successful take place in a blaze of passion and publicity, this notoriety is more a function of the public's fascination with the downfall of the mighty than of the uniqueness of the occurrence. Self-defeat is actually an equal-opportunity disorder that, more often than not, goes undetected until severe damage is done.

A number of self-defeating strategies flourish without detection because they appear well intentioned. For example, if you adhered strictly to the motto of either the U.S. Marine Corps—*Semper fidelis* ("Always faithful")—or the Boy Scouts of America—"Be prepared"—your actions might well result in patterns of self-defeat. The following two clinical cases typify the self-defeating dynamic that involves too much of a good thing.

One patient was an attorney who suffered what might be called a semper fidelis pattern of self-defeat in his relationships with women. Jeffrey was a senior partner with one of the most respected law firms in the country when he entered therapy with a complaint of chronic impotence—but only with his wife. When he worked with his legal secretary or met her for after-hours dinners, however, he could not only achieve a full erection but also could reach orgasm several times by masturbating (alone) after the meeting. Despite the severe frustration this state of affairs precipitated, he steadfastly refused to have any sexual contact with his secretary (despite her urging)—or any other woman, for that matter. He believed that his wife was "an angel who could be the ideal mate (sexually) if only [he] would learn how to behave with a *real* woman."

When Jeffrey entered treatment, it was his sixth attempt at initiating psychotherapy for distress over his sexual dysfunction and the negative self-image he derived from not knowing how to gain his wife's approval. He had aborted each of his previous starts with therapists, because he felt it was inappropriate for them to examine the disordered relationship that he and his wife had forged. After two sessions it was clear that he firmly believed—and could not be shaken from the contention—that if he behaved in an exemplary manner, he could secure tender love and affection from a spouse who was obviously treating him in a cold, controlling, and highly critical manner. Moreover, he maintained that once he secured respect and caring from his wife, their sex life would be idyllic.

In all other aspects of his life, Jeffrey was a superachiever. He had been valedictorian of his high school class. He had graduated *summa cum laude* from an Ivy League university after being elected to Phi Beta Kappa. At his top-ranking law school he had made the law review. As an attorney, he was earning over $500,000 a year and had just been voted "Man of the Year" by a local civic organization. Although childless, he gave time and financial support to several charities devoted to the needs of disadvantaged youth.

The only cause that this man could not serve was his sexual self-interest. Although some might suggest that the man could qualify for sainthood, his virtue—particularly his fidelity to a cold, cruel spouse—was clearly a self-destructive vice. His behavior was self-defeating because his attempts to correct his disordered relationship with his wife, while possibly an effective means of gaining approval in other contexts, had proved over years of trials to be a grossly ineffective tactic that required intensive psychotherapy.

The attorney's case of severe self-destructive behavior can be contrasted with a far less debilitating pattern of self-defeat whose motto might be "Be prepared." While practice does make perfect, overpreparation for difficult or anxiety-provoking tasks—often a form of chronic procrastination—can qualify as self-sabotage. In the case of Richard, a fairly intelligent, unmarried thirty-three-year-old man who hoped to become an opera singer, preparation clearly violated the fundamental tenets of the pleasure principle.

When Richard first entered psychotherapy, he reported that he had gone through a modest inheritance by paying for spe-

cialized voice coaches and training that he hoped would pre-
pare him for a solo career with an opera company. In fact, it
was only the largesse of a rich uncle that was now enabling him
to continue with his voice coach and enter psychotherapy; he
borrowed all the money he needed for his daily living expenses, because his training left him no time for a job. This
man did nothing other than to train his voice; he felt that being
a singer would afford him the flair or élan that his bland
existence lacked. Before embarking on his self-defeating regimen, he had been a high school gym teacher and had found
time to date occasionally, but he had given up all social activities while pursuing his dream of becoming the next Pavarotti.

Although the aspiring singer's self-defeating behavior was in
no way comparable to that of the self-punitive attorney, it was
nonetheless maladaptive. He never received any impartial encouragement to continue with his operatic studies, never fared
well at an audition, and never received extraneous rewards
(such as making new friends) from trying to join an opera
company. On the contrary, his "preparation" for the career of
his choice had left him penniless, socially isolated, and psychologically dejected. What had begun as the pursuit of a life-
enhancing dream had continued well past the point at which
this would-be singer should have thrown in the towel to avoid
suffering losses difficult to recoup. By preparing excessively, he
never needed to stop and acknowledge his limited talents.
Once again, this is a case of a virtue—in this case, persistence—becoming a self-destructive vice.

It is important to recognize how often ostensibly normative
behaviors qualify as instances of self-defeat. People with advanced university degrees, fully aware of the dangers, refuse to
wear seat belts while driving. The same type of self-defeating
denial is shown by pregnant women who smoke or drink
alcohol, as well as by people with a susceptibility to skin cancer

who refuse to wear sunscreens or protective clothing while exposed to the sun. Deeply bronzed self-defeatists are often called sun worshipers, but given the potential hazards associated with their behavior, the term *thanatophiles*—after the Greek word for "death"—might be more appropriate.

Other self-saboteurs, particularly among the young and the gifted, ignore public service announcements describing the dangers of engaging in casual sexual contacts without condoms, despite their awareness that AIDS is an incurable disease. Although many see the failure to practice "safe sex" as a form of impulsiveness that has been around since the dawn of humanity, in the 1990s lack of self-restraint is far more consequential than it once was. Consider the tragic fate of Earvin "Magic" Johnson, who, according to his own account, had unprotected sex with dozens of women because he believed that catching the AIDS virus could never happen to him. It may be unfair to say that all unsafe, impulsive sex acts are self-destructive, but when patterns of such acts emerge over time, it is appropriate to call the behavior self-defeating.

Sex is not the only sphere of self-defeat for young people. Consider Adam, a young man who by age fifteen had managed to get himself expelled from four preparatory academies despite having a straight-A average. Each expulsion would follow the same scenario: He would pay a holiday visit to his father, a man with three advanced degrees whose primary passion was to see his son become an academic success. Adam would return to school either drunk or overtly under the influence of a psychoactive drug such as cocaine. The next morning he would pick a verbal fight with one of his teachers, and the battle would end up in the headmaster's office. This routine did not always lead to his dismissal from school—authorities were tolerant of this boy because of his obvious intelligence and their sense that something was psychologically amiss—

but he would repeat the pattern until eventually his father was summoned and told that the boy was being expelled. The pathetic predictability of the boy's behavior marked it as clearly self-destructive.

SELF-DEFEATING BEHAVIOR: THE TRAGIC PARADOX

Given the array of examples we have presented so far, it is fair to ask what we mean, precisely, by *self-defeating behavior*. The term is not easy to define, because so many different actions have the potential for self-defeat. Moreover, the concept and several related ones (such as masochism) have been discussed by so many people in so many different ways that it is hard to arrive at an unequivocal definition. The essence of self-defeat, however, is bringing harm, loss, failure, or suffering to oneself through one's own actions or inactions. It is the opposite of behaving to further one's best interests.

The "self" in *self-defeat* refers not just to the physical body but also to the self as a meaningful or symbolic identity. Thus, self-defeat can mean not only hurting yourself physically, emotionally, or mentally but also damaging your reputation or interpersonal relationships. Moreover, we extend the notion of self to include personal goals and projects. To thwart yourself from reaching the career goal that you dreamed of (given *some* objective basis for expecting success) is thus to commit self-defeat, even though no physical or mental harm has occurred.

We have called self-defeat a tragic paradox because it seems to violate the essence of rational action and natural behavior. Nature instills in us the urge for self-preservation, and rational thought shows us how to reach our goals, starting with satisfaction, health, comfort, and pleasure. Simply put, being rational means analyzing and pursuing our own best interests. Self-defeat is thus fundamentally and essentially irrational. It is this irrationality that fascinates psychologists, because it suggests that deeper, darker motives can overcome the normal and sensible ways of acting.

The human tragedy of self-defeat lies in the sad or painful outcome that people bring on themselves. Just as tragedy, in the purest sense, is more than mere misfortune, self-defeat is more than suffering. After all, no one's life is filled exclusively with joy, pleasure, and success; some measure of suffering or failure is to be expected as an unavoidable part of the human condition. Self-defeat, however, seems fully avoidable. You can't help it if your plans are dashed by luck, the weather, or a determined rival. But if you yourself are the cause of your downfall, it is hard to avoid thinking that it didn't have to end that way. To have your plans thwarted by your own actions is a cruel irony indeed.

Any definition of self-defeat must also emphasize the total outcome of the behavior, and not just the occurrence of harm or suffering. In our view, actions qualify as self-defeating only if the harm or loss outweighs the pleasure or benefits. It is normal and rational to expect some measure of unpleasantness in the pursuit of many desirable goals, and the goals make it worth it. For example, joggers suffer fatigue and aching limbs in the interest of health and fitness, dieters suffer deprivation and hunger in order to achieve an attractive physique, and ambitious workers accept the loss of leisure time in the pursuit of long-range career goals. None of these is necessarily a pattern of self-defeating behavior, although any of them could qualify if you ultimately came to feel that the gains had not been worth the sacrifices. It is thus the balance between positive and negative outcomes that is decisive.

Another key issue is intentionality: Is self-defeat intentional?

We have much to say on this point later, for it is far from simple. Still, one large and important class of behaviors— namely, pure accidents—must be ruled out right from the start. True, people do sabotage or harm themselves accidentally, but we are not going to go into the psychology of accidents. This book is devoted to exploring *intentional* actions. We are not restricting our focus to destructive intentions per se, but the actions must be intentional even if the self-destructive outcome was not foreseen.

Consider, for example, the case raised by a member of the audience at a lecture given by one of the authors. He described how his aunt had electrocuted herself trying to vacuum up the snow from her sidewalk. In a literal sense, this accident would qualify as self-destruction, insofar as the woman was the cause of her own death. Yet nothing would be gained by stretching our focus to encompass cases such as hers. She simply didn't understand electricity, and she didn't follow the safety instructions that came with the vacuum cleaner. Had she known the dangers and nonetheless decided to take the risk of vacuuming snow, then we might properly say she was engaged in self-defeat, but she didn't.

Another phenomenon that we exclude from our discussion is suicide. As the literal and ultimate act of self-destruction, suicide might at first appear to be a prototype of self-defeat. Closer inspection, however, suggests that suicide follows principles and patterns that differ markedly from the forms of self-defeat that pervade ordinary life, and it is the latter that concern us.[8]

In this book we use several terms other than *self-defeat* interchangeably, including *self-sabotage, self-harm,* and *self-destruction.* These are to be regarded simply as synonyms for *self-defeat.* One term we do not use, however, is *masochism.* In its original and correct usage, *masochism* refers to a pattern of sexual behavior in which whipping and humiliation are used for sexual stimulation. Sexual masochism is not self-destructive, because masochists are not out to harm themselves; they merely use pain or deprivation to facilitate their pursuit of pleasure and satisfaction.[9] By and large, sexual masochists know what they want, they pursue it, and they are happy with the outcome, so there is no basis for regarding their actions as a form of self-defeat.

Another reason for avoiding the use of *masochism* as a synonym for *self-defeat* is that the term has become politicized. Because of a misunderstanding of sexual masochism, theorists, beginning with Freud, have used this term to suggest that the sufferings of some unfortunate victims (especially women) stem from some innate propensity to enjoy harm. Although the view that masochism is peculiarly female is now largely discredited, the term still justifiably arouses feminists' sensitivities. Given the political baggage, conceptual confusions, and misleading connotations, we think it would be best if the term *masochism* were restricted to its original, sexual meaning.

One other area we do not cover is compulsively self-injurious behavior. Some people engage in seemingly random patterns of banging their heads against walls or hard objects, biting themselves, pinching or scratching their own skin, slapping their own faces, or consuming dangerous substances. Such patterns of behavior occur almost exclusively in cases of severe pathology or retardation and do not generalize to the rest of the population.[10] Again, we devote our interest to the broad variety of self-defeat in everyday life.

WHY DO PEOPLE DO THESE
THINGS?

As we have seen, people find all kinds of ways of behaving in opposition to the pleasure principle. In view of this variety, we may well wonder whether a single common drive or motivation can account for these superficially dissimilar acts. To state the question another way, Is it possible to reduce all self-defeating behavior to the pursuit of one fundamental gratification, as psychiatry has attempted to reduce all behavior to the pursuit of pleasure and minimization of pain? We think not, but ours is, to date, a minority opinion, particularly among psychiatrists.

Freud may have met his professional Waterloo when he attempted to explain the paradox of self-defeating behaviors. In fact, the dynamics of self-defeat seemed to perplex and disturb him so intensely that in a 1924 paper he asserted: "If mental processes are governed by the pleasure principle, so that avoidance of 'pain' and obtaining pleasure is their first aim, masochism [his catchall term for self-defeating acts] is incomprehensible."[11] Self-saboteurs also apparently threatened Freud on a personal level. After acknowledging that he could not make sense of their behavior, he went on to note: "In this light, masochism appears to us as a great danger, which is in no way true of sadism, its counterpart."[12] It may seem odd that the father of modern psychiatry would be more disquieted by people who direct aggressive impulses inward than by those who target them toward others; but in fact, most people—laypeople as well as mental health professionals—share his judgment.

Freud's difficulty in coming to grips with self-defeat is evidenced by the fact that over time he advanced three distinct theories to account for it. In fact, he often presented conflicting viewpoints on the functions or consequences of self-defeating behavior (he called it either "masochism" or "moral masochism") within the same paper.[13] Freud was inclined to view patterns of self-defeat as part of our genetic makeup. He often allowed for the fact that pain-seeking behaviors—typically those that symbolically reenact past traumas—could have an adaptive function as well. Yet he appeared to favor attributing self-sabotage either to the action of "Thanatos," a death instinct that operated in opposition to "Eros," the drive to maximize pleasure and minimize pain, or to what he conceptualized as the influence of "characteristically female" predispositions.[14]

The multiple formulations Freud used to account for self-defeating behavior merely hint at the range of explanations that have been advanced to account for this fundamental paradox. Most, if not all, of these explanations attempt to be all-encompassing—and in so doing, fail miserably. For example, one of the more widely held explanations for self-defeating behavior follows Freud's theory of "erotogenic masochism."[15] This theory, a cornerstone of psychoanalysis, maintains that self-focused aggressive, hostile, or destructive impulses derive from a failure to resolve the Oedipal conflict between a child's innate sexual desire for the parent of the opposite sex and the fear of being punished by the same-sex parent (by castration) for having such feelings.[16] Freud argued that self-punitive acts could alleviate the anxiety-ridden guilt that arose from Oedipal urges by "paying the price" for pleasure. In other words, children were allowed to indulge in fantasy if they traded a self-imposed beating for the feared castration.

The obvious concerns posed by this unverifiable theory were magnified considerably when the concept was extended to "moral masochism." Freud and like-minded psychoanalysts believed that a variant of erotogenic masochism operated in adult life and accounted for various failures to achieve academic, vocational, or interpersonal success. They argued that success of any stripe, be it graduation, marriage, or reaching the pinnacle of one's profession, represents or recalls an Oedipal victory: a child triumphing over the same-sex parent to assume the prized sexual/romantic position with the parent of the opposite sex. As we have seen, such a victory carries with it the debilitating fear of retaliation from the more powerful same-sex parent. Unless we have successfully resolved the Oedipal conflict by relinquishing the desire for the opposite-sex parent to seek a lover of our own, the theory argues, residual guilt for the fantasized vanquishing of the same-sex parent will cause us to sabotage adult successes in order to preempt, symbolically, the feared retaliation. In so doing, we supposedly preserve a known level of safety in return for giving up the potential rewards of success.

The adherents of this Oedipal guilt model of self-defeat never fully address one fundamental assumption that, left unexplained, severely undermines their theory: that individuals somehow have the foresight to barter self-inflicted suffering of known intensity and duration for potentially more intense pain meted out by someone else according to that other person's timetable. Further complicating the task of explaining all kinds of self-defeating behaviors with psychoanalytic theory is the fact that most occur without benefit of success and may, in fact, be precipitated by punishing events and failures.

TOWARD A MORE VIABLE
EXPLANATION

Psychoanalytic models of self-defeat are intriguing and often valuable in understanding certain self-defeating syndromes, and we look at several of them more closely in the chapters that follow. For example, in attempting to account for self-defeating behaviors, Freud maintained that the normal lives of neurotics revealed a tendency to pursue fates that would always lead to some form of psychological suffering. Dubbing this phenomenon a "repetition compulsion,"[17] Freud identified one type of self-defeating behavior known to figure prominently in the lives of those who were victimized in childhood and suffer revictimization throughout their adult lives.[18] In general, however, such models fail tests of pragmatism. When we look at the consequences of the behavior instead of the supposed antecedents, we can often find more parsimonious explanations for self-defeat: if self-inflicted pain can be seen to have rewarding outcomes, it seems unnecessary to posit Oedipal conflicts as the cause of a self-defeating syndrome.

We believe, in fact, that all formulations attributing the realm of self-defeating behaviors to one-dimensional drives, motives, or reinforcement histories are far too narrow and wholly inaccurate. Self-sabotage comes in a variety of distinctive forms. To see self-defeat as a by-product of unresolved rage that can only be directed toward an abusive parent symbolically through an embattled marriage may explain cases like the Hands or George and Martha, but how can this dynamic provide insight into the ill-advised strivings of Richard, the would-be opera singer? Other theories that attribute all self-defeat to the influence of guilt may account for certain instances of successful people who hit bottom after attaining goals that somehow feel ill-gotten, but how does such a force allow for the case of Jeffrey, the selectively impotent lawyer? Recall that he had achieved success in several realms of his life and was potent when apart from his wife, but he failed to perform in one unique arena—the marital bed. Is it not more logical to assume that other factors precipitated his selective failures? We believe so. Rather than attempting to reduce all instances of self-defeat to a common cause, we acknowledge the *multiple styles of self-defeat* that exist while trying to account for the unique motives underlying them—a necessary and scientifically appropriate stance.

A Continuum of Self-defeating Patterns

Earlier in this chapter we defined self-defeating behavior in terms of deliberate, intentional actions. The fact that the actions were intentional does not mean, however, that the destructive consequence was intended. People intend to gamble, for example, but they don't intend to lose all their money. The issue of how much the person intended the destructive consequences or even just foresaw them is crucial for understanding any particular pattern of self-defeat. In fact, it is quite useful to distinguish self-defeating patterns along a continuum ranging from deliberate, intended self-sabotage to largely unforeseen self-harm occurring as an unwanted by-product of other actions.

One basis for understanding this continuum of self-defeating behaviors is the foreseeability of harm.[19] At one extreme, people deliberately take actions that will clearly and definitely bring harm to themselves. At the other extreme, people do not foresee the harmful consequences of their actions. They want to avoid negative outcomes, but they act in ways that sabotage their own efforts to reach positive, desirable goals. In the middle of the continuum are patterns in which people may foresee the possibility of harm but ignore it or downplay it. Looking back, they may recognize that the bad outcomes were foreseeable and avoidable: I knew I should have worn my seat belt or used (or had my partner use) a condom or quit smoking or not gambled all my money. At the time, however, they ignore those risks and dangers and look instead to the good that may come. In other cases, the bad outcomes may be foreseeable and avoidable but may be accepted as trade-offs for psychological benefits.

The continuum of self-defeat may also be examined in terms of the healthfulness of what someone is trying to accomplish. When self-harm occurs once as an unforeseen, unwanted by-product of our efforts to pursue normal, healthy goals, there is little or no reason to stigmatize us as maladjusted or mentally ill or unstable. On the other hand, when self-harm occurs in the context of irrational, ill-advised, or destructive motives, then concern about our adjustment and mental health is warranted. In other words, the self-defeatist must be judged on the basis of the motives, not the outcome, of the behavior. To decide whether someone is pathologically self-destructive, it is necessary to examine what he or she was trying to accomplish, not just what was accomplished.

The element of risk makes the distinction between intent and outcome especially clear. As we shall see, a significant portion of self-destruction arises because people do risky things. They are not seeking self-harm—in fact, they hope to avoid any harm—but they accept risks that turn out badly. They might have done the same thing and avoided the bad outcome: not everyone who smokes gets lung cancer, and some people never wear seat belts but never have accidents in which they are injured. In our view, it is appropriate to include such cases of happy endings under the rubric of self-defeating behavior.

If one may speak of self-defeating patterns even where there is no harmful outcome, then the converse must also hold true: some actions should not be regarded as self-defeating even if there is a destructive result. The ordinary driving of a car might fall into this category. Some people who drive cars in a cautious, safe, lawful fashion, taking defensive precautions and maintaining vigilance, end up killed in an automobile accident. There seems no reason to label these people as self-destructive. The odds seemed to be on their side, and they acted rationally and prudently. In other words, in judging the self-defeatist, we must consider the motives—both conscious and unconscious—behind the behavior, not the outcome alone.

Thus, judging self-defeat requires looking beyond the outcomes of an act. It is necessary to appreciate what was foreseen and intended to understand what was done in the context of the actual circumstances. Not all harm is self-defeat, nor do all self-defeatists suffer from their actions.

THE VARIETIES OF SELF-DEFEATING BEHAVIOR

As we have described, we see self-defeating behavior on a continuum of intentions and foreseeability of harm. Along that continuum, we identify three broad styles of behavior.

Well-intentioned Self-defeating Behavior

Some self-defeating behaviors are directed at the attainment of healthful goals and outcomes. People who exhibit these types of behaviors are judged to be self-defeating for two reasons. First, they chronically employ ineffective approaches to attain their goals, and second, over time they fail to change or correct their ineffectual behavior, even when they recognize that the course of action they have embarked on is not succeeding. The person who engages in this response style does not foresee negative consequences at the outset but ultimately suffers pain because he or she either lacks the resources needed for the task or is using the wrong resources to achieve a healthful goal.

One of the most common patterns of well-intentioned self-defeating behavior is perseveration, in which the old adage "If at first you don't succeed, try, try again" is carried to a pathological extreme. The would-be opera singer introduced earlier in the chapter was doing just that. He apparently did not have the talent to succeed in opera, yet he persisted in pursuing his goal when a realistic appraisal would have shown that his chances of reaching it were nil. People who exhibit well-intentioned self-defeating styles like this cause themselves pain because their goal-directed activities do nothing to sustain or enhance their competence image. Like rodents on exercise wheels, "going nowhere fast," they undermine or destroy their chances of feeling productive—one of the two outcomes considered by most to be the defining features of psychological health (the other is love).

Perseveration is often the cause of self-defeating love relationships. Recall Jeffrey, the "impotent" attorney who persisted in pursuing his wife's affection despite opportunities for alternative sources of gratification. He failed to act on an overwhelming body of evidence that his romantic pursuits were in vain; and by adhering to a pattern of behavior proven to be unrewarding, he deprived himself of a gratifying love relationship and caused himself intense pain and suffering.

Perseveration is by no means the only form of well-intentioned self-defeating behavior. A number of other pat-

terns that involve misjudgment in pursuit of a healthful goal
are described in chapter 2. In addition, there is a form of
behavior known—especially in the sports world—as choking.
Here, the problem is not that one is trying the wrong approach
or trying too long but that one is trying too hard. We consider
that phenomenon in chapter 3.

Self-serving Self-defeating Behavior

People who engage in well-intentioned self-defeating behavior wind up losers. They have gone after a desirable goal but
achieved nothing. In another broad style of behaviors, however, the self-defeating behavior serves a more obvious purpose. Although it inflicts harm or suffering that is clearly
foreseeable, it also provides immediate benefits, such as relief from a psychologically aversive situation. When people
choose to accept an unfavorable cost-to-benefit ratio that involves inflicting self-harm (typically felt in the future) in
order to protect their self-esteem or their public image of
competency in the present, they are engaging in self-serving
self-defeat.

Undoubtedly the most common form of self-serving self-
defeat is substance abuse. Alcohol, tobacco, and virtually all
recreational drugs have been shown to harm physical health,
and most users are aware of the potential costs. Yet many
people easily ignore the long-term potentially destructive effects in return for immediate pleasurable sensations and relief
from distress.*

---

*We do not intend to downplay the role of socioeconomic or sociocultural forces
in predisposing certain people toward substance abuse, nor do we discount the role
of biochemical, genetic, and other physiological factors in initiating and sustaining
patterns of substance abuse and/or addiction. We consider these factors to be

Alcohol in particular has been found to serve the needs of self-serving self-defeatists in two different ways. On the one hand, research has shown that alcohol reliably reduces the noxious state of consciousness known as objective self-awareness.[20] In heightened states of self-awareness, people become more cognizant of who they are and how well they measure up to standards of competence, social status, or similar values.[21] Their focus shifts from external concerns, such as what is going on around them, to themselves; and they see themselves as in a photograph that accentuates all the warts, moles, and other blemishes that mar the ideal image valued by society. On a bad day—after failing a test, ending a relationship, or passing a milestone without having realized our dreams—conscious self-awareness can be a highly aversive state. Alcohol can help to lower self-awareness by blotting out undesirable thoughts and shifting conscious attention from the self to extraneous concerns.[22] The self-destructive aspects of this behavior pattern are obvious. Short-term emotional relief comes at the cost of increased risk of long-term physical and social costs. By failing to address the factors that make objective self-awareness aversive, the drinker merely forestalls an inevitable confrontation with painful reality.

A second major appeal of alcohol as an agent of self-serving self-defeat is a tactic known as self-handicapping.[23] This term was coined to describe a pattern of self-protective behavior that uses impediments to success to enable a person to preserve a favorable competency image. By heightening the likelihood of failure today, the person preserves a self-image that

---

independent of the psychological forces that motivate people to engage in systematic patterns of self-defeating behavior, however. Thus, while we acknowledge that substance abuse is a common consequence of a number of forces, in this book we address only those aspects having a direct bearing on our model of self-defeating behavior.

holds out the promise of success tomorrow. The self-destructive aspect of self-handicapping is, of course, that the behavior may actually precipitate real failure.

Self-handicapping strategies work like this: A person with a highly favorable competency image arranges to report for a test of his or her ability under the influence of an agent known to inhibit performance—often, but not always, alcohol. Judgments of the person's inherent, underlying competence to perform will be confused by the actions of the handicapping agent. Recall the case of Eugene Fodor, for example. When his performance failed to meet the expectations established by his award-winning past, observers could never reliably determine whether the decline was due to a falloff in competence or to the inhibitory effects of drugs.

In essence, self-handicapping means hampering the functioning of one part of the self (for example, coordination) to protect the image of another, more valued part (such as innate competence). People who use this self-defeating strategy relieve the immediate anxiety of being exposed as less able, worthy, or talented than had been assumed in exchange for the potentially negative consequences. They may comfort themselves with the promise that someday, when the effects of the handicap have worn off, their competence will again be manifest. Moreover, as we saw with Deschapelles, if the self-handicapper succeeds in spite of the handicap, attributes of the person's underlying competence will soar. We say more about this "augmentation effect" in chapter 5.

Substance abuse is, as we have noted, a common self-handicapping strategy, but it is by no means the only one. A number of the public figures mentioned earlier in this chapter—from government officials like Gary Hart and Wilbur Mills to religious leaders like Jim Bakker and Jimmy Swaggart and financial superstars like Ivan Boesky and Michael

Milken—can be seen to have been using self-handicapping behavior to preserve or enhance their competence image. In chapter 5 we examine some of the other ways that self-defeatists have found to handicap themselves in pursuit of psychological gains.

Maliciously Intended Self-defeating Behavior

At the far end of the continuum of intentions and foreseeably negative consequences are the patterns of malicously intended self-defeating behavior. These patterns have no healthful intent and inflict foreseeable harm both to the self and to others. In fact, this self-defeating style is almost always immediately interactive: maliciously intentioned self-defeatists regularly establish long-term relationships with others who enable them to ⅍ act out the pattern repeatedly, often actually helping to inflict the harm suffered by the self-defeatist.

Maliciously intentioned patterns are the most overtly irrational form of the fundamental paradox of self-defeat. Although, like other patterns of self-defeat, they may yield transient psychological benefits, the overwhelming distress caused by the angry acts typical of this dynamic obscures any benefits from conscious awareness. The behavior presumably is reinforced and maintained by the temporary relief of psychological conflict, but the manifest consequences of this self-destructive style are hostility and aggression directed inwardly and at someone else.

Some people who engage in maliciously intentioned self-defeating behaviors appear to be perennially "looking for love in all the wrong places." A prototype of this pattern is the character of Terry Dunn in Judith Rossner's *Looking for Mr. Goodbar,* who repeatedly subjects herself to dangerous and abusive relationships while rejecting other relationships in which she could have found love.[24] In contrast to the persevering attorney who, as his marriage soured, engaged in a grossly ineffectual attempt to right what went wrong, people like Terry Dunn go far beyond choosing or holding on to a less-than-gratifying relationship; the hallmark of their maliciously intended self-defeating behavior is that they provoke a spouse or lover to reciprocate hostilities on a one-to-one basis.

Ralph and Olivia Hand, described earlier in the chapter, typified this self-defeating style. Throughout their volatile marriage, they abused each other, then made love, divorced, then made love, got into drunken brawls, then confessed their undying loyalty to each other—a pattern that probably would have continued had Mr. Hand not killed Mrs. Hand. If there were psychological gains to either party, they are unknown to us; certainly there were no ostensible benefits. What we can say with great certainty is that on both sides the behavior was clearly maliciously intended. Mr. Hand wed a woman who was as abusive as he, if not more so. It is therefore safe to maintain that he was not self-handicapping; he could derive no protection of or enhancement to his self-esteem from the handicap of his cruel spouse. It is also relatively easy to conclude that Mrs. Hand's self-destructive behavior was devoid of self-protective intent, since she had returned to her hometown to marry Mr. Hand immediately after suffering both career and marital failures. Self-defeating behavior can be judged to protect self-esteem only when it either follows success that is psychologically disruptive or seeks to ward off threats to a highly favorable self-image.

The most overtly aggressive self-defeating style is what we call Pyrrhic revenge (named after the Greek king Pyrrhus, who won a battle over the Romans by sustaining excessive losses). Its essence is an attempt to harm oneself in order to strike out

at someone else. It is clearly distinguished from all other manifestations of self-defeat by the fact that it cannot be construed
as promoting good health. A self-handicapper may rationalize
taking a drink before a performance by saying that it will calm
his nerves, and an abused spouse may see staying in a bad
marriage as an act of humanitarianism or economic self-
preservation; but no amount of distortion can deny the de-
structiveness of acts of Pyrrhic revenge. People who indulge in
this type of behavior do intend to hurt themselves, but that is
not their primary objective; they want to hurt someone else in
the process.

Because maliciously intentioned self-defeating behavior
rarely occurs in a vacuum or without an enabling partner,
members of the psychoanalytic community have dubbed this
style *sadomasochism.* This term implies—correctly, we believe
—that self-defeat may be used to gain symbolic, psychological
victory or control over another. For the same reasons that we
have rejected *masochism,* however, we have found *sadomasochism*
inaccurate and misleading. Phrases such as "the weapon of the
weak"[25] or "victory through defeat"[26] seem preferable to describe the unique substyle of maliciously intended behavior
that we call Pyrrhic revenge. People who employ it achieve a
psychological victory over others in much the same way as
boxing legend Muhammad Ali achieved victory over his opponents during the later phase of his career, when his strength
and skills were waning. Ali's "rope-a-dope" technique, in
which he would lean on the ropes and weather the punches
until his opponent was exhausted, enabled him to outlast and
outsmart other boxers and occasionally even to win bouts.

Pyrrhic-revenge strategies often seem to enable self-
defeaters to vanquish tormentors in a similar manner. They
enable a person to adopt a "holier-than-thou" posture, not
stooping to the level of the other person's assault and instead

accepting the tormentor's abuse.[27] And moral superiority aside, they give the self-defeatist a psychological advantage, weakening or defeating an abuser by not falling after taking that person's best punch—real or psychological.

The Pyrrhic-revenge strategist thus causes psychological harm by rendering impotent someone who seeks dominance over him or her. Because this strategy does not involve actively inflicting harm on another person through physical or verbal assaults or abuse, it is an effective way to retaliate symbolically against, for example, the abuses meted out by parents in years past. Without personally acting as an aggressor, you can hurt them by defeating their aggressive actions or intent. Recall the boy who, despite his academic successes, was thrown out of one prep school after another. His father, who held several advanced academic degrees and highly valued education, would berate him each time for "bringing shame, humiliation, and suffering" on the family and on his "forebears, who are unquestionably spinning uncontrollably in their graves." In psychotherapy, the boy revealed that he had relished the sight of his father suffering with him as he sabotaged his own education. In chapter 6 we examine in more detail how self-defeatists may use Pyrrhic revenge to reenact childhood abuse in an attempt to gain mastery over a situation that had been beyond their control during their formative years.

A LOOK AHEAD

Thus, self-defeating modes of behavior, when viewed in terms of the intent of the behavior and the foreseeability of negative consequences, can be understood as widely diverse, with more variety than commonality. In general, people who exhibit one mode of self-defeating behavior tend to stick with it over time and do not shift from one mode to another. For that reason, our goal has been to identify characteristic styles of self-defeating behavior, rather than particular types of self-defeatists or specific developmental histories that might be responsible for particular self-defeating syndromes. Although we later suggest likely origins of the various self-defeating styles, we do not intend to suggest a one-to-one correspondence between patterns of self-defeat and events that preceded them. We believe that a person's characteristic mode of dealing with the world results from a combination of many psychological, interpersonal, and societal forces. We want to help readers understand the consequences of exhibiting a self-defeating style, regardless of how or why it emerged.

In the chapters that follow, we demonstrate in more detail the intricate dynamics of the self-defeating behavioral styles we have identified and explain why self-defeatists never win. Even presumably "mild" patterns of self-defeat, if left unchecked, can result in a syndrome that can lead to self-inflicted demise. In the final chapter we offer a number of applications for our model of self-defeat and emphasize early intervention. We look at the ways in which parents, educators, employers, and spouses can identify self-defeating styles and alert sufferers to their repetitive patterns of behavior before the behaviors become irrevocably destructive. The conflicts, anxieties, and expectations that drive self-defeatists *can* be short-circuited.

2

When Good Intentions Backfire

All in all, we can't help concluding that the main cause for the defeat was that we had become conceited with past successes.
—Rear Admiral Motomo Ugaki, the chief of staff to Admiral Gombē Yamamoto, on the Japanese navy's disaster at Midway, often seen as the turning point in the Pacific theater in World War II

AS we begin now to examine self-defeating patterns and processes up close, we start with several of the milder patterns, those identified as well-intentioned self-defeating behavior. Although the modern fascination with self-destruction tends to invoke dramatic images of sweeping catastrophes and sinister motives, leading to the permanent devastation of careers and families,[1] the everyday reality of self-defeat is often mundane, pathetic, and even laughable. The story of self-defeat may indeed end in tragedy, as discussed in later chapters, but the beginnings of self-defeat sometimes lie closer to comedy.

Consider this recent news item: Joseph Meyer, a salesman, pulled into a service station–convenience store one evening to buy cigarettes. He saw a man eyeing his car in a suspicious way, so he waited until the other man had walked past. Then Meyer went into the store—and left the motor running and the lights on. Not surprisingly, he came out to see his car being driven away. He went back into the store, phoned the police, and then went to a nearby agency to rent a car.

After driving home, he began to dial the number of the cellular phone in his own car. At first there was no answer, but after about forty tries the thief answered, and Meyer began to negotiate to get his car back. The thief wanted $500; Meyer did not have that much on hand, so they haggled for several hours. Finally they agreed on a price around $300. Meyer wanted to come pick up the car right away and asked where they should meet. The thief gave the address of a bar, but he did not want to meet there; so he said he would call back in about half an hour with instructions on where to meet him.

Meyer agreed and hung up. He then called the police, updated them on the car theft, and told them where the thief was. The police could hardly believe the story, but they went to the bar and, sure enough, there was the car. Shortly thereafter the thief came out of the bar, was arrested, and taken straight to jail.[2]

Were Meyer and the car thief self-destructive? Consider their actions. They both made decisions involving foreseeable risks that led to major setbacks for them. Meyer, despite seeing a suspicious character, left his keys in the car and the motor running, making it easy to steal his car. The thief revealed his location to his victim by telephone, leading the police to arrest him. Of course, there is no reason to think Meyer or the thief deliberately sought misfortune. Nor, in this case, did their misfortunes attain epic proportions: Meyer had his car stolen but eventually recovered it, and the thief was arrested but probably did not spend much time in prison. Still, these two men did bring misfortune on themselves as a direct result of their actions.

This, then, is the first category of self-defeat. People are guided by ordinary, comprehensible motives, but they do things that bring setbacks and problems to themselves, including failure, misfortune, distress, and other difficulties. Often they are seeking normal, rational goals, but they choose means that bring about unhappy outcomes that are not at all what they intended or wanted. In this chapter we explore how such things happen.

One key is misjudgment. People misjudge themselves and their circumstances, and these errors in judgment lead to self-defeat. People may overestimate what they are capable of achieving, they may misperceive what is possible and probable, or they may ignore certain decisive aspects of their situations.

Misjudgment may seem too mundane or trivial an explanation for self-defeating behavior, especially for someone taught to expect to find self-destructive desires deeply rooted in human nature. But although death wishes, desires for perverted pleasures, and other such self-destructive desires are an appealing theme for literature or movies, in everyday life there is little evidence of them. In a recent search of the extensive research literature about normal human behavior, the researchers wanted to find out whether normal people ever do self-destructive things.[3] The answer: People do bring failure and suffering on themselves, but *failure and suffering are rarely or never their goal.* There was no evidence to support the theory that modern American adults are driven by self-destructive impulses or desires. Even guilt does not appear to create a wish for punishment. Rather, as we have noted in chapter 1, self-destruction occurs as an unwanted by-product of efforts to attain positive, desirable goals.

PERSEVERATION: MISGUIDED PERSISTENCE

A first and important self-defeating pattern is misguided persistence. Banging your head against a wall will not get you through the wall, and persisting only damages your head more without improving your chances of success. Such persistence is also referred to as perseveration. Often reflecting crucial judgment errors, it can lead to a great deal of harm and loss.

At first it may seem ironic for us to identify excessive persistence as a mechanism of self-defeat. Persistence, of course, is often regarded as a virtue. People praise those who persevere and eventually triumph despite initial setbacks and obstacles, and they belittle those who give up too easily. Americans have no use for quitters. Western folklore extols the one who perseveres, from the "little engine that could" of the children's story to great innovators such as the Wright brothers or Robert Fulton, the inventor of "Fulton's folly," the steamboat. There is even a sympathetic smile reserved for members of such groups as the International Flat Earth Society, who refuse to believe that the earth is round.

Realistically, though, persistence is not always for the best. Some plans, approaches, or strategies simply do not work, and persisting at them simply multiplies the number of failures. The American tendency to idolize persistence disguises the fact that it often leads nowhere.[4] An investor may stick with a stock whose price has dropped, only to find that it continues to drop, so he ends up losing even more money. A scientist might be working with a theory that's simply wrong; if she keeps basing her experiments on it, they will continue to fail, and she may miss out on a successful career. A football coach may get disastrous results every time he calls for a blitz or a screen pass; if he keeps trying those plays, he may end up losing the game (and his job). If a student has no aptitude for math but takes numerous math courses, she probably will get lots of low grades.

In other words, it is important to know when to quit. The truly adaptive virtue is not blind, automatic persistence in response to every failure but rather the ability to make an accurate judgment of when persistence will pay off and when it will not.

Spouse Abuse and Self-defeat

A far more tragic and important manifestation of persevera- tion in relationships involves battered wives. The case of Fran- cine Hughes is well known, largely because of Faith McNulty's nonfiction account of it, *The Burning Bed,* and the subsequent Farrah Fawcett movie of the same name. At age sixteen, Fran- cine married Mickey Hughes, a young man who soon became physically violent and abusive. Her life with him was a saga of beatings and rages that continued for over a decade, during which she suffered terribly. Frequently the small family (for they had several children) was evicted for failing to pay rent, and Mickey's absences ranged from overnight disappearances (for drinking binges and sexual infidelities) to brief periods of incarceration. Francine had many opportunities to leave him and in fact did leave him several times, but she always returned. She divorced him but soon resumed living with him and supporting him financially. Later, looking back, she acknowl- edged that she could and should have left him and stayed away, but she kept returning to him when he apologized and prom- ised to reform. She thought that if she could act in the right way, she might be able to prevent him from beating her. The relationship ended only when, after receiving a beating followed by sexual intercourse, she poured gasoline all over the floor of the bedroom in which he was sleeping and set fire to the house. Mickey was killed in the fire. Instead of finding herself free, however, Francine was indicted for murder; and to avoid a long prison term, she had to convince the jury that she had temporarily gone insane.

For decades now, battered wives have been the victims not only of their abusive husbands but also of psychological theorists who, in insulting and condescending analyses, have portrayed them as, among other things, masochistically orchestrating their own suffering in order to satisfy some deeply buried desire for punishment. However, close study of these women rarely supports the conclusion that they want to suffer, nor do battered wives get any apparent satisfaction from the brutal treatment inflicted on them. There is nothing in the story of Francine Hughes to suggest that she wanted to suffer or received any satisfaction from being hurt. In fact, she got nothing but pain and humiliation from her victimization.

Fortunately, recent work has gradually disproved these stigmatizing, victim-blaming theories and replaced them with a more sympathetic view. Battered wives do not want to be battered. But freeing them from the diagnosis of self-destructive intent or masochism does not necessarily mean that they have no self-defeating patterns at all. In fact, battered wives—and battered husbands, for that matter—are often engaging in patterns of behavior that reflect self-destructive intent. From our perspective, Olivia Hand and Martha the female protagonist from *Who's Afraid of Virginia Woolf?*, whom we described in chapter 1, were both enacting self-destructive syndromes other than those that can be explained by misguided persistence when they repeatedly engaged their husbands in brutal battles. As we detail in chapter 6, their pattern of incurring horrible injuries within the context of an ongoing relationship demonstrates that self-defeating acts can gratify hostile or aggressive impulses. On a more benign level, there can indeed be an element of self-defeat in the battered wife who keeps returning to her husband and believing his promises to change his ways. Once or twice, perhaps, it might be reasonable to believe that an abusive spouse erred in some way that can be avoided in the future, but when the abusive behavior conforms to an established, chronic pattern, or when multiple episodes of battering have occurred, it should be apparent that the future will not be all that different from the past. Francine Hughes eventually came to realize that her husband would continue to drink, waste money, and beat her.[5] In such cases, to keep returning to an abusive spouse is to accept a substantial risk of further mistreatment. Yet some women do, as the Hughes case shows.

What is self-defeating about such choices, however, is not any desire for suffering or satisfaction in mistreatment. The self-defeating element is a pattern of poor judgment, of choosing to persist in a bad relationship. When we look at the problem in that way, we can perhaps understand how some women will make these mistakes. They have, after all, invested a great deal of time and effort in the relationship, probably because there have been some good periods too, and it is emotionally difficult to throw away the positive legacy of intimacy that has been achieved during the good times. Furthermore, the abusive spouse may be sincerely repentant each time, and his promises of better behavior may be heartfelt—he sincerely intends to stop hurting her. In reality, of course, he lacks the self-control and other traits that would enable him to fulfill these promises, but he does not realize this, and the woman thus has to be able to see the truth despite his entreaties.

Francine Hughes certainly conformed to these patterns.

There were good periods in the relationship, although they became briefer and rarer. Her investment in the relationship was substantial, beginning with her dropping out of high school and having her first sexual experience with Mickey and then building as the couple had children. Mickey's apologies were often spoken with conviction and feeling, and they were often followed by significant improvements in his behavior, although only for a while. On one occasion when Francine seemed quite serious about leaving him, Mickey even joined a church and Alcoholics Anonymous, convincing her that she should try again to make the relationship succeed.

Many women who become victims of abusive spouses have low self-esteem, which can contribute to problems of perseveration. When there is some understanding in advance that persistence may lead nowhere—that the situation may be a dead end—people with high self-esteem are sometimes able to size things up more quickly than people who lack self-esteem. High self-esteem enables such people to say, "This is getting me nowhere" or "Things are only getting worse, not better," so they may be able to pull out of the losing situation sooner than other people.[6]

High Self-esteem and Persistence: Not Panaceas

High self-esteem is no cure-all either, however, because it may even increase fruitless persistence in some cases. People with high self-esteem may be confident that they can achieve success eventually, and therefore they may meet failure with increased determination, harder efforts, and other marks of persistence. Most laboratory studies have found that people with high self-esteem persist longer in the face of failure than people with low self-esteem, probably because they simply believe that they will eventually succeed.[7] In particular, people who think very well of themselves tend to persist even in situations where they are given the sound advice to quit and move on if they do not succeed immediately.[8] Because of their high self-esteem, they tend to be reluctant to listen to advice, preferring to rely on their own assessment and their inner confidence. They also seem to have difficulty believing that they could really fail, so they keep on trying. Only when they realistically consider the possibility that a situation or problem may be impossible are they better than people with low self-esteem at making the right decision and pulling out of a doomed endeavor.[9]

Parenthetically, we are reminded of how inaccurate the notion that "nothing succeeds like success" can often be. Apart from breeding arrogance and a sense of narcissistic entitlement, succeeding in an endeavor often closes one's mind to constructive alternative approaches to problem solving that can be invaluable during times of stress. A report in the *Wall Street Journal* describing the travails of Digital Equipment Corporation's founder and CEO, Kenneth H. Olsen, identified precisely how success can breed self-destructive contempt for novel ideas. According to this report, Mr. Olsen, a founding father of the computer industry, had known all about the development of personal computers long before they reshaped the field of high technology, but he had dismissed the PC as a "toy" rather than a challenger to the mainframe computers he had helped develop.[10]

The key, then, is whether people fully appreciate the fact that persistence can lead to futility and frustration. An unthinking belief in the efficacy of persistence can be very harmful, whereas a careful assessment of when to persist and when to quit can yield the best results. We are not suggesting that persistence is uniformly bad; we are simply saying that it is not uniformly good.

To put this another way, the key to success is not simply determination and persistence and refusal to be a quitter, but an accurate assessment of yourself and the world. Knowing what is possible for yourself in a given situation is vital.

FREUD ON PERSEVERATION

As we saw in chapter 1, the Freudian perspective on self-defeating behavior is an unwieldy composite of explanations ranging from a death instinct to the biological predispositions of females to unresolved Oedipal guilt. Interestingly, however, Freud did advance one perspective on perseveration that many psychotherapists find quite useful: the so-called "repetition compulsion."[11] Mental health professionals have actively embraced this perspective because it helps explain why certain people replicate patterns of self-defeat with all the significant people in their lives—particularly their psychotherapists.

Freud maintained that when certain events overwhelm underdeveloped childhood egos, traumatized people will often repeat the event in their minds—through dreams, fantasies, or obsessions—in an attempt to master through imagery what could not be mastered physically. He argued that many people who suffer these repetition compulsions will also symbolically "act out" their attempts at mastering a trauma in some portion of the real world—ideally, with a psychotherapist. Thus, a young boy traumatized by a brutal father may, according to Freud's reasoning, dream or fantasize about vanquishing the father as a form of repetition compulsion. If this mechanism fails and the trauma is left unresolved, the boy might find as he grows into adulthood that he "inexplicably" becomes involved in a number of relationships with men who mistreat or abuse him.

Repetition compulsion theory holds that by unconsciously

getting involved in one abusive relationship after another, this young man would be trying to use adult representations of his traumatic involvement with a brutal father to seek vindication for past humiliation, pain, and suffering. He would persist with attempts to correct a failed relationship despite obvious indications that his efforts were doomed to failure. Freud said that only within the context of an effective therapeutic relationship could such a traumatized person recognize the origins of his conflicts and ultimately master them.

A massive body of research confirms the contention that rather than ultimately resolving trauma or exacting retribution, repetition compulsions actually make psychic wounds worse.[12] People who suffer traumatic victimization in childhood suffer consistent revictimization—at ever-increasing levels of harm to the self—if their wounds are left untreated. According to one researcher, victims of child sexual abuse regularly become prostitutes, pornographic models, or victims of marital violence.[13] As predicted by repetition compulsion theory, women who were abused as children and who do not receive psychotherapeutic care often spend a lifetime involved in relationships that reenact the sexual violations that originally traumatized them.

A Different View: Self-esteem

While we see the value of using the idea of repetition compulsion as a way to account for and address many of the more difficult interactions that occur within psychotherapy—such as a hostile transference, in which a patient treats the therapist as a disliked parent—we also find that this construct can muddy the explanatory waters when it comes to evaluating the myriad behaviors that appear to be instances of self-defeating perseveration. For example, Jeffrey, the impotent attorney described in chapter 1, would appear to be enacting a repetition compulsion in the context of his marriage. His mother was, in his words, "a cold, withholding bitch"; thus, there is some logic in assuming that his attempts to be "good enough" to win his wife's love are a replication of his striving for academic success during childhood in order to win his mother's love. If one evokes the concept of a repetition compulsion as the sole mechanism for understanding this attorney's behavior, however, why was he not cruel to his wife? If his mother withheld love and hurt him by doing so, why did his repetition compulsion not lead him to retaliatory behaviors that would rectify the emotional damage done to him in childhood? Moreover, why would the attorney fail to have affairs with available women either as a means of symbolically balancing the scales of justice so rudely tipped by his wife's hostility or merely as a rewarding escape?

One way of accounting for Jeffrey's failure to seek alternative modes of gratification lies in his reinforcement history. As we noted in chapter 1, Jeffrey was a superachiever in a variety of performance arenas. His maladaptively high sense of self-esteem—at least as it pertained to his capacity for securing emotional gratification—may have prevented him from realizing that you cannot master interpersonal relationships in the same way that you manifest competence in vocational pursuits. In fact, the commonsense notion that corporate CEOs and superachievers in fields ranging from sports to science fail to secure gratifying romantic involvements can be accounted for in the same way.[14] By misapplying in the context of intimate relationships the skills that they use to secure vocational rewards, many successful people like Jeffrey defeat themselves by failing to realize that they are persisting in behaviors inappropriate to the task at hand and consequently doomed to failure.[15]

If we reject the repetition compulsion analysis and focus

instead on the research suggesting that high-self-esteem people refuse—or do not know when—to give up, we have a parsimonious way to explain the self-defeating behavior of this man: he is a stellar professional success who never really learned a health-promoting way to deal with failing at a task he set out to master. Such an approach does not rule out the possibility that other forces are contributing to the problems. Once his self-defeating symptoms have been arrested, many conflicts, including sexuality concerns and repressed hostility, may surface and can be dealt with directly.

At this point we should repeat that we do not advocate one explanatory mechanism over all others for understanding self-defeating behavior. Our intent here in contrasting a Freudian interpretation of Jeffrey's pattern of self-defeat with a self-esteem formulation is to drive this point home. The goal of our analysis is to help clarify the operations or methods of self-defeatists as they behaviorally contradict the pleasure principle, not to search for the psychological seed or virus—the motive—responsible for their paradoxical behavior. Such an endeavor would itself be self-defeating.

WHY NOT JUST CALL IT QUITS?

Persistence, then, is not a virtue but a tool, only beneficial if used properly. Otherwise, it becomes useless or worse: perseveration, a means of self-defeat.

The dangers of perseveration are perhaps most vividly illustrated in people's tendency to throw good money after bad, a tendency amply documented.[16] Once people have invested a certain amount of time, energy, cash, or other resources in some project, they become reluctant to abandon the effort, and as a result they may squander a great deal more on a losing project—they become too heavily invested to quit. Another common expression is "knee deep in the big muddy"; you are reluctant to turn around and back out after you've already gotten dirty, but going forward may simply sink you in deeper.

In one laboratory study of responses to bad investments researchers found that 87 percent of investors persisted past the optimal point. In fact, over half of them persisted past the break-even point—the point at which their net return *even if they were to succeed* would have been less than their initial stake.[17]

It is easy to sympathize with the dilemma people face when they have spent money (or time or energy or emotion or other precious resources) with little to show for it except additional demands. To back out is to admit failure and to guarantee that all you have invested so far is lost. But to persist is to risk even more on what may ultimately turn out to be a failure. You hope that further investments will finally bring success that will make the entire project seem worthwhile. But all too often, that hope leads simply to greater and greater failures.

The same difficult choice is faced by a government that has poured millions of dollars into a problem that seems only to be getting worse. The American government's "war on drugs" of the 1980s was a vivid illustration. Each year there were more calls for more money, and the failure of these expenditures to bring progress—by most accounts, things were getting worse—simply stimulated calls to spend even more. The same kind of logic applies when lives are being spent instead of, or along with, money. A government that has sent thousands of its young men to their deaths in a military venture finds it hard to write them off and abandon the undertaking. Indeed, late in the Vietnam War, George McGovern ran for the presidency and promised to pull

American troops out of Vietnam immediately after taking office. Yet the American public overwhelmingly rejected his plan, preferring instead the vague promises of Richard Nixon and Henry Kissinger to negotiate a peace that would at least offer some benefits to show for all the blood and treasure America had expended.

What Will Other People Think?

To appreciate the dilemma is not, of course, to minimize the self-defeat that can result from making the wrong choice. What, then, are the causes of counterproductive perseveration? One important factor is a feeling of personal responsibility for the initial decision. The person who made the initial decision is much less willing to write it off than someone who comes from a neutral, unbiased standpoint.[18] That is, the original decision maker feels responsible for what has gone wrong and therefore wants to persist and make it come out right. To use the preceding example, it might have been possible for a new president to decide just to pull out of Vietnam, because that president would not yet have made any decisions to commit substantial resources. For a person in Nixon's position after having presided over the war for several years, it would have been much harder to withdraw.

Moreover, if the initial decision was made in the face of opposition, the decision maker is even more likely to want to persist despite failure.[19] To withdraw is, in a sense, to admit that the initial investment was a mistake. It is generally hard for people to admit mistakes, but it is especially hard if they have to admit them in the presence of someone who advised against them beforehand. To put it another way, people may dislike hearing someone say, "You blew it," but they posi tively detest enabling someone to say, "I told you so." And so, ironically, having a vocal opposition may make it harder for us to change our minds to do what the opposition advocates.

The concern with what other people say and think is indeed important in self-defeating perseveration. We may persist against our better judgment simply to avoid being called quitters. In one study researchers examined persistence as a function of what the subject thought the onlookers would think of each decision and found that people's decisions were strongly swayed by the desire to look good. If the audience disparaged giving up, then the subject tended to persist. But if the audience favored discontinuing, then persistence was much lower.[20] It is not surprising that people want to look good to others. The important point, though, is that such motives affect even decisions about such things as investments and reassessments of commitments. The decision about whether to persist is not simply a rational appraisal of expected gains versus losses, for concerns over saving face can override such rational considerations.

The issue of rationality is important, because as we have noted, self-defeating behavior is in a sense the ultimate irrationality. Research has shown that if people are induced to stop and make careful, accurate, detailed calculations of all the probable costs and benefits, they are less likely to become entrapped in a cycle of misguided, destructive perseveration.[21] People *can* often avoid the perseveration trap if they make decisions cautiously on a logical, rational basis. Self-defeating perseveration thus occurs not because people are *unable* to make the best decision but because they *refrain* from making the best decision. They base their decision on the wrong criteria, such as saving face or sustaining emotional momentum.

Choosing by Doing Nothing

The use of inappropriate decision criteria is perhaps most vividly illustrated by one other factor that has been shown to influence perseveration: passivity. With many choices in life, doing nothing results in a particular course. This course is called the passive option, and people apparently tend to choose the passive option—whatever it is—often. Anyone who wants to influence people can use this principle to elicit compliance. For example, many mail-order book or music-album clubs use the passive option to increase sales. Each club member or subscriber receives a catalog with a featured selection each month and must take some action to refuse the featured selection. If the customer does nothing, then the company automatically ships the featured selection and bills the customer for it. In other words, the passive option is to make a purchase, and companies find that this arrangement results in higher sales than the more conventional system where the company simply sends out a catalog and waits for the customer to place an order—a system that makes a non-purchase the passive option.

Clinically a passive option can be an incredibly powerful, albeit disordered, option. A major form of character disturbance known as a passive aggressive personality disorder has, as its defining feature, a pattern of passive resistance to demands. As research on this phenomenon has shown, not responding can be a powerful mechanism for securing demands in the short run, but it ultimately leads to a variety of harmful outcomes over time.[22]

Persistence decisions often involve passive options, and it appears that people tend to favor the passive option there, too. Sometimes people have to take action in order to persist, such as by sending in more money. In other cases, persistence itself is the passive option, such as in holding on to your stocks and hoping that they will increase in value. People persist more under the latter arrangement than under the former.[23] Thus, a kind of psychological inertia—a tendency to do nothing when choices could be made—can contribute to this form of self-defeating behavior.

In short, self-destructive perseveration seems to arise from poor, lazy, or improperly based decisions. These often involve overestimation of oneself, excessive concern with oneself (including the concern with making a proper impression on others), or decision making through passivity.

OVERCOMMITMENT AND OVERCONFIDENCE

Having considered fruitless persistence, we should now back up and consider the making of commitments in the first place. Sometimes the self-defeat is not in the persistence but in the initial decision. Most commonly, people go wrong by taking on too many obligations. They overcommit themselves in ways that can lead to stress and disaster.[24]

Taking on Too Much

Even if it were possible to go through life without getting involved with anyone or anything, it would probably not be desirable to do so. Involvements bring most of the joys and satisfactions that enrich life; they also bring obligations and demands. Making commitments is thus a kind of trade-off, and indeed we could conceivably treat overcommitment as a self-defeating trade-off rather than as a counterproductive strategy. We have chosen to include it here because it often seems to follow the pattern of misjudging oneself and the world and hence selecting a strategy that backfires.

For example, take the case of Frieda. This young woman knew what she wanted: a satisfying and successful career as a clinical psychologist. To achieve her goal, she needed to gain admission to a graduate program in that field, which was difficult because most such programs receive hundreds of applications for a handful of positions. Frieda's application at her chosen university was rejected.

Because she lived near the university, she decided to try a strategy that had worked for other people in similar circumstances. She would enroll as a nondegree student at her own expense in a few courses and thus prove to the faculty that she was a desirable prospect. Then she would reapply for admission to the program.

Frieda's error, however, was in deciding which courses to take. She decided she would prove her worth to herself and others by taking a course in the area where she was weakest—statistics. She also selected one of the most challenging courses in the program and, to round things out, the introductory course for that clinical graduate program. At the end of two semesters, she had achieved a B in the introductory course and C's in the other two courses. Graduate students are not supposed to do C work, so those grades looked very bad. All she had accomplished with her year's work was to accumulate evidence that she was *not* qualified for graduate school. To be sure, she had received the C's in difficult courses, and occasionally students within the program also received such grades. But Frieda was trying to prove that she deserved to be admitted, and she had failed to secure any positive evidence that she could perform well. By choosing the difficult courses, all she did was achieve an ambiguous failure, whereas an ambiguous success (such as an A in an easy course) would have helped her cause far more. Her reapplication was rejected and, when we last heard from her, she was rethinking career plans.

People also overcommit themselves outside of the school and work spheres. A common pattern with credit-card purchases lands people deeply in debt. They buy things that they want and run up large bills that they cannot pay. As a result, they have to spend a significant amount of their monthly income paying interest charges on the bills, often at rates approaching 20 percent per year. In a study of working-class people, one researcher asked many of her interviewees what they would do if they suddenly received a great deal of money such as from a lottery or a surprise inheritance. Almost invariably, they said that they would first pay off their bills—an answer that indicated their keen awareness of their own oppressive debt.[25]

Of course, it is hard to reproach individuals for falling prey to such burdensome indebtedness when the United States is doing the same thing. When this chapter was written, a news analysis had pointed out that all the income taxes paid by every American citizen in the western half of the country, from the Mississippi River to the Pacific Ocean, were needed simply to pay the interest on the national debt. No goods, no services, no aid to the poor, no funds for research, no weapons, no salaries for all the government employees, no aid for the farmers or disaster victims, no support for school systems, and so forth—all that money was simply poured into servicing the debt.

Nor is financial overcommitment limited to the working class and the government. The super-rich make similar errors, too, despite their vaunted fiscal savvy.[26] The 1980s saw the fall of financial titans such as Robert Campeau and the Reichman family, who both made their money in real-estate developments and other related enterprises. They were too confident in the power of their immense wealth, and they invested aggressively in a wide variety of ventures. Both ended up with heavy losses and nationally visible embarrassments, symbolized by having to sell off large parts of the financial empires they had built.

A related pattern involves having children.[27] Nearly everyone wants to have children, and America's vision of the good life includes a happy family complete with cute, smiling youngsters. But people who have too many children or have them too early in life find that their lives and marriages can suffer. When a husband and wife have little opportunity to enjoy each other's company, the relationship may never develop fully, or it may simply degenerate into sullen mutual resentment. The stresses and strains of parenthood, such as worries, fears, and sleeplessness, may be compounded by the unforeseen expenses. Of course, children do bring pleasure and satisfaction as well; our point is simply that having too many children, or having them before you are ready, can be self-defeating.

Always Looking to Win

The patterns of overcommitment, especially those involving errors such as the grandiose schemes of Campeau and the Reichman family, may arise from overconfidence. Although Americans applaud confidence, it, like persistence, has its dangers too. Often confidence does help people perform well, and it would be absurd to suggest that confidence is generally or universally a bad thing. But overconfidence can cloud judgment and lead people to commit themselves to goals and projects that are beyond their reach.[28]

In fact, confidence may be an important factor in some

patterns of persistence that we noted earlier in this chapter. We saw that people with high self-esteem are prone to make the error of persisting too long in a losing endeavor because they refuse to accept failure. And even people like Francine Hughes, who said her self-esteem was very low throughout her abusive marriage, can have signs of overconfidence in some areas. In an effort to make sense of her marital catastrophes, Hughes concluded that "her fault lay in overestimating her strength."[29] She had thought she could make the marriage succeed and could make whatever sacrifices were necessary. That misplaced confidence kept her in a cycle of continuing, escalating abuse and conflict that brought her years of suffering and eventually led her to kill her husband.

Historical examples of the perils of overconfidence abound, ranging from Napoleon's invasion of Russia to the stock market crash of 1929.[30] Recently, the psychologist Shelley Taylor and her colleagues have argued that mental health and well-being are linked to positive illusions—that is, the tendency to see yourself and your prospects through a rose-colored lens of favorable distortions.[31] Although such pleasing distortions may help people feel better and perform better, they can be a risky basis for judgments, decisions, and commitments. That is, being full of optimism is fine and perhaps even desirable when getting up in the morning, performing your duties, or relaxing with loved ones. But excessive optimism can be dangerous when you are deciding how much money you can afford to bet at the racetrack or invest in the stock market.

The ideal situation, perhaps, is to be able to turn off these positive illusions when making judgments and then to turn them back on to enjoy the emotional benefits. Some evidence suggests that people can do this under some circumstances.[32] That is, some people can walk around most of the time in a pleasant haze of optimism but can abruptly become coldly rational and clear-sighted when sizing things up for a major decision. On the other hand, there is also evidence that this ability to turn self-deception on and off is fragile. People do allow their egotism to influence their decisions, and the common inflations of egotism can lead them into regrettable decisions and excessive commitments.

It'll Never Happen to Me

A particularly relevant—and particularly dangerous—form of positive illusion has been labeled the "illusion of unique invulnerability."[33] People are especially optimistic about what can and will happen to them personally, and as a result they tend to believe that bad things will mainly happen to others. Therefore, they may take chances or act in ways that can expose them to great dangers.

The illusion of unique invulnerability has thus been linked, for example, to sexual behavior.[34] Sexual activity carries great risks of unwanted pregnancy and deadly disease. If people take precautions, they can minimize these risks. But people who succumb to the illusion of unique invulnerability often fail to take these precautions, risking outcomes that could alter their life plans and even bring death. The role of overconfidence in teenage (or other unwanted) pregnancy is familiar, and research confirms its continuing relevance.[35] Its role in the AIDS crisis has also been established. As warnings about the dangers of AIDS and its modes of transmission became public, people continued to have unprotected, promiscuous sex, even in places such as gay bathhouses where the deadly virus seems to have spread rapidly.[36] Indeed, some people said that fear of AIDS caused so much stress that they went to gay bathhouses more often, because orgiastic affairs helped take their mind off their worries![37]

In 1991, Magic Johnson, the basketball superstar, acknowl-edged that he had tested HIV-positive and apparently had become infected through unprotected heterosexual inter-course. Investigators soon discovered that players—especially star players—in the National Basketball Association had ample opportunities for sexual adventures, and some players apparently took full advantage of these opportunities without bothering to protect themselves from the potential dangers. Stars may be especially prone to overconfidence of this sort, in part because their extraordinary successes make them think that ordinary rules and contingencies do not apply to them.[38] Johnson's announcement sobered many people, partly because it ostensibly showed that no one can plan on beating the odds. Yet even such an obvious example seemed to lose its power to dispel the dangerous illusion of invulnerability of many players. Less than three months after Johnson's public an-nouncement, one NBA trainer was quoted in the news with this assessment of its effects: "Guys were worried for about a week, then went back to doing what they were doing."[39] George Andrews, Magic Johnson's agent, said that he had not noticed any lasting change in players' postgame habits, and he observed, "It's a situation where people still don't think it can happen to them. After the initial shock wore off, things went back to normal."[40]

Given the excesses reported about the jet-set life—from the drug-overdose deaths of Jim Morrison and John Belushi to the sexual exploits of athletic superstars like Wilt Chamberlain, who boasted of having bedded more than 10,000 women—self-destructive arrogance should top the list of perils known to derive from achieving stardom.

Even if people are not particularly overconfident, they can still overestimate their prospects by misperceiving their situa-tion, with potentially tragic results. For example, after a popu-lar outcry and upheavals had led to the election of legislative bodies that took control of France in the late 1700s, King Louis XVI retained very little power. He did have some prerogatives and veto rights, but he was largely a figurehead. His wife, Marie Antoinette, urged him to take her and their children and flee the country. The king, however, saw no reason to flee. He replied that they had already done everything to him that they could possibly do; things could not conceivably get any worse. And so he stayed. Contrary to his prediction, things got considerably worse; and when he did decide to try fleeing, it was too late. He and his wife were both publicly executed under the guillotine.[41] His overconfidence consisted simply in believing that things were as bad as they could get, when in fact things were capable of getting far worse.

LEARNED HELPLESSNESS

Sometimes people develop self-defeating patterns after they have failed or experienced setbacks—even minor ones. Consider Gloria, who had never liked computers and had avoided learning to work with them. In college she eventually had to take a particular course that required some computer work. There was no way out of it. Plucking up her courage, she went to the computer-terminal center at the library. The center supervisor took her to a terminal, gave her a brief explanation, and showed her how to turn the machine on and get hooked into the mainframe computer. As the connection was established and the files opened, the supervisor felt that Gloria was now all set, and he moved on to help someone else as she inserted into her terminal the diskette containing her data.

Unfortunately, at just that moment, a problem developed across campus at the main computer center. It had nothing to do with Gloria or anyone else in the library, but Gloria had no way of knowing this. All she knew was that as soon as she inserted her diskette into the machine, her screen went blank, as did the screens of everyone else in the room. It didn't help matters that the supervisor turned back to her immediately and asked, in a loud voice, "What did you just do?" Everyone else in the room looked at her too. She thought that somehow she had broken the entire university computer system.

Of course, Gloria had done nothing of the kind, and when the supervisor called the main computer center, the problem was quickly cleared up. But it may have been too late for Gloria. Her attitudes about computers were crystallized that day, and even when friends explained to her that inserting her diskette could not possibly have destroyed the computer network, could not even have caused that temporary breakdown, she was not about to try again. The unfortunate coincidence had taught her that she was helpless and incompetent with computers. If she had simply tried a few more times to learn, she might well have discovered that computers are not all that difficult and mysterious and that she, like thousands of other people, could indeed learn to make the computer work for her. But she was not about to try.

Gloria's case provides an illustration of the kind of phenomenon psychologists have called learned helplessness.[42] Earlier in this chapter we saw that optimism and overconfidence can be self-defeating, but the other side of the coin is that pessimism and lack of confidence can lead to just as destructive an outcome. Learned helplessness typically arises when a series of defeats or setbacks cause people to adopt a passive, withdrawn attitude that makes them prone to give up easily. As the label implies, people seem to learn that they are helpless. Learned helplessness can be a self-destructive pattern, for the person fails to learn or achieve or succeed even when conditions become favorable. Gloria *could* have resumed work and learned how to operate the computer effectively after the temporary breakdown was fixed, but by then she was no longer open to learning.

The phenomenon of learned helplessness was discovered by psychologists studying how animals acquire patterns of behavior. In one common paradigm for studying learning, dogs were placed in a box with a partition in the middle, and an electric current was run through the metal grid on the floor. The dogs received shocks and would typically run around until they happened to jump over the partition to the other side, where there was no shock. On the next trial, the dogs would start off with the same frantic response but would tend to jump across the partition faster. After a few more trials, the dogs would simply wait by the partition and jump to safety as soon as the shock began. In fact, if the shock was preceded by a warning tone, the dogs could learn to step nimbly across the partition as soon as the tone sounded, thereby avoiding any discomfort. This is a familiar, well-documented pattern of avoidance learning.

In one experiment, however, researchers did something else first. They restrained the dogs and gave them shocks from which there was no escape. When these dogs were then put in the box with the partition, they never learned to hop over to safety. Even if researchers dragged the dogs over the partition as if to show them how to escape, the dogs would not learn. Apparently, the dogs had learned that there was nothing they could do to escape from the shocks, and they stopped trying or learning. The dogs had become helpless.[43]

Learned helplessness apparently occurs far less commonly among people than among lower animals, for people often seem to develop beliefs and expectations that enable them to ignore failure and try again.[44] Usually, when people experience failure or frustration, they try even harder. When the vending machine takes your coins but gives you no merchandise, you probably don't just stand there numb and helpless. Most likely, you press the buttons a few more times (harder!) and yank on the coin-return button. You might even try to slap or tilt the machine to get your item. People tend to respond to an uncontrollable situation by trying harder to control it.

Eventually, of course, people do give up.[45] Repeated or escalating experiences of futility eventually make people act helpless, even to the extent that they will fail to try or learn in a subsequent situation. It is thus not the single experience but the long history of failure that is most likely to create a condition of helplessness.[46] Even the case of Gloria, described earlier, involved more than the single dramatic problem on that one day: she had felt insecure and mistrustful around computers for a long time.

Social Contexts and Learned Helplessness

If there are significant numbers of people in our society who have learned to be helpless, then, they are likely to be found in circumstances that repeatedly and systematically have offered them no chance to exert any control. Victims of poverty or discrimination may eventually stop trying. The cycle of failure, apathy, and low self-esteem that seems to mar many inner-city residents' lives could be a product of circumstances that teach people to see the American dream and promise as a hoax. Indeed, such a pattern may be the most disturbing and insidious consequence of the long history of racial discrimination. Nowadays there are many opportunities open to minority people because of widespread, aggressive affirmative-action programs. The apparent failure of minority members to take full advantage of these opportunities is a source of perplexed disappointment to many thinking and caring citizens and policymakers. Part of the explanation may be that many people simply do not believe that the opportunities exist. Individually or in groups, they may have concluded long ago that they will not be given a fair chance, so they are not going to try.

This pattern of learned helplessness may help explain one curious feature of American society. Foreign visitors and observers sometimes express surprise that recent Asian immigrants have fared so well in America. The success of these people seems to call into question the claim of blacks that whites want to reserve power and wealth for themselves. But such a juxtaposition may be unfair to blacks precisely because of past experience. Many Asians have arrived here recently with high hopes, energy, and faith. They are able to work confidently toward their own version of the American dream. It is probably much harder to muster up so much optimism and drive if you start off with a belief that your efforts will be futile.

In an important way, the contrast between the success of Asian immigrants and the travails suffered by blacks points to our concern with considering the context of symptoms before forming judgments about their self-defeating intent. As we discuss throughout this book, any symptom—from abusing alcohol to tolerating spouse abuse—must be assessed within a context that includes an analysis of the antecedents that precipitate a behavior as well as the consequences of the behavior, in order not to overattribute blame to the victim's character.

Obviously, many factors contribute to the problems of race relations and prejudice.[47] We are not suggesting that learned helplessness is the sole answer, but it may well be part of the picture. People who have accumulated a long sequence of experiences of failure and futility are probably the ones most prone to feel and act like the helpless animals in those laboratory studies.

People who are seriously ill and incapacitated also undergo experiences that may induce helplessness. Some hospital procedures are especially pernicious in fostering helplessness. When the medical crisis begins, there is nothing patients can do, and they must submit passively to others' ministrations for a long time. Only after the others have completed their work do the patients take charge of their own recovery. By then, the psychological difficulty may have become great.

For example, people who experience a heart attack or stroke must allow the physicians and nurses to save their lives. Surgery and intensive care occupy the first days and perhaps weeks. When the danger is past, however, the patient must then take charge of developing a proper exercise plan and implementing any suggested regimens for therapy, but many people have difficulty shifting from the enforced passivity back to a more active role.

Elderly people in particular have to come to terms with being unable to do many things they were once accustomed to doing. A series of research studies has dramatized some of the problems they face. One well-known study compared the responses of institutionalized elderly people to various circumstances. Some had everything done for them, while others were assigned responsibility for their own care. Those who were put in the more active role recovered better and survived longer.[48] Indeed, people who had been randomly assigned the duties of caring for a houseplant fared better than other people in the same institution who had no such responsibility.

These findings created a stir because they fly in the face of traditional beliefs about quality of care. It had long been assumed that the best form of care involved doing as much as possible for the patient, and the most expensive nursing homes attempted to be as thorough as possible. But, ironically, patients may be better off in a place where they have to do some things for themselves. The active exertion of control seems to have benefits, whereas patients may soon become helpless if everything is done for them.

Interpreting Failures

Learned helplessness, when it occurs, seems to depend on how people judge themselves and the world. In particular, if people interpret failure as reflecting something stable about the self, then they will probably expect to fail again, and this interpretation makes it very difficult to try again.[49] In contrast, the same failure may not bring any helplessness if the people can blame it on external factors or see it as an isolated misfortune. This contrast points to the way that personality traits render an individual vulnerable to engaging in this form of self-defeat. A person's style of drawing conclusions and making interpretations about success and failure may be an important clue. Thus, certain people may be prone to become helpless if they are generally inclined to blame themselves for their problems and to see their problems as stable and wide-ranging.

In sum, learned helplessness is a matter of giving up too easily, and it seems to be based on a low evaluation of the self. Some evidence even suggests that high self-awareness can be a cause, at least as a factor that makes people more vulnerable to learned helplessness.[50] Focusing on yourself as deficient seems to be an important source of harm.

INTERPERSONAL STRATEGIES
THAT DON'T WORK

Two additional forms of counterproductive self-defeating strategies can be found in interpersonal behavior: ineffective bargaining strategies and ingratiation strategies that backfire.

Striving to Be Liked

Ingratiation strategies are things people do to be liked. The desire to be liked is deeply rooted in human nature, and nearly everyone performs some actions to win the liking of others. Some of these actions may backfire and become self-defeating, however. Ironically, people do not want others to do things simply in order to secure their liking. This reaction creates what researchers have dubbed the "ingratiator's dilemma": the ingratiator tries to act in a way that will win the other's liking, but if this motive becomes apparent, the actions will fail.[51] To get others to like you, you have to do the things that will appeal to them, and you must convince them that you are not doing those things in order to get them to like you. In other words, ingratiators must conceal their true motives.

When people fail to win the liking of others, the ingratiator's dilemma often plays a prominent role. For example, flattery is a common means of ingratiation, but people of low status gain little by flattering those with high status. Telling your boss that you think he or she is wonderful, brilliant, fair-minded, and wise will most likely come across as a transparent bush-league ploy, and it may even induce your boss to begin regarding you as a shameless manipulator. Still, studies show that people with low status continue to use ingratiation anyway, often eliciting predictably negative reactions of their superiors.[52] In short, the tendency of people to flatter their betters is often self-defeating.

Likewise, doing favors for people is usually effective at promoting liking, but it can occasionally backfire and create negative, self-defeating reactions. In particular, people dislike the sense of obligation that a favor can create.[53] One of the authors was once having dinner in a college dormitory when a female friend mentioned that she had been asked out on a date and was uncertain what sort of obligation (for example, sexual) she would feel if she accepted. When told that first dates do not normally carry much obligation, she added that the fellow was rather wealthy and the first date would involve a trip to Italy for a week! Despite the appeal of such a trip, she decided not to go out with him. Thus, by trying to do too great a favor, he elicited a negative reaction.

Blunders in Bargaining

Bargaining is an ancient art, although the optimal or perfect strategy has not yet been found. Even though we humans have not pinpointed a single correct strategy, we have at least identified some incorrect and ineffective ones. Recent studies have revealed several common approaches that produce negotiation failure. These are the fixed-pie approach, aiming too low, and aiming too high.

The fixed-pie approach is probably responsible for the majority of bargaining stalemates.[54] This approach is based on the fallacious assumption that there is a fixed, limited quantity of resources to be divided up. Sometimes, of course, that is the case, but at other times additional alternatives can be found— ones that enlarge the pie, in effect. Many creative compromises rest on the discovery of just such alternatives. Otherwise, the negotiation tends to get bogged down on one particular issue, and both sides become inflexible.

For example, a salary dispute may remain unresolved as long as both sides insist that their final offer is indeed final, and it may well be the case that neither side can afford to make further concessions. As long as the discussion focuses exclusively on the salary argument, there may be no progress. But by introducing other issues or options into the discussion, it may be possible to find a common ground. Part of the salary could be offered as performance incentives, so that management's risk is reduced. Or additional benefits, services, or vacations could be provided to improve the package to the workers without corresponding cost increases to management. More generally, a tendency to regard the bargaining situation as a conflict between opponents may lead to stalemate. Viewing the relationship as a partnership may help resolve some issues.

Aiming too low is perhaps the most obviously fallacious approach to bargaining.[55] People may underestimate the strength of their position and therefore make unnecessary concessions, ending up with a poor outcome. An accurate appraisal of your own position as well as of the other person's position is therefore central. For example, if you fail to appreciate your value to an employing organization, you may not make strong enough demands regarding salary and benefits. You may fail to realize how easily you could get another job or how difficult it would be for your employer to replace you.

Even if you do have an accurate sense of your own priorities and needs, failing to discern the vulnerabilities in your opponent's position may also cause you to aim too low. For example, a woman may approach a divorce negotiation thinking that her top priority is to get custody of the children and her second priority is to have a fair share of the money. Her husband may contest the custody decision, and when he finally begins to yield, she may be so relieved that she will settle for a smaller share of the financial resources. But in many cases his interest in having the children may be much smaller than hers, and his pursuit of them may have been merely a bluff. If she had offered to relinquish custody in return for a greater share of the resources, he might have capitulated. In other words, if having custody of the children is highly desirable to one person and not very desirable to the other, then whoever recognizes this imbalance is likely to fare better in the negotiation. Evidence suggests that after divorce most men experience a significant increase in their standard of living, resume dating, and soon remarry, all of which would be greatly hampered if they had custody of the children. By simply trying to get something that is of little value to the other side, one may aim too low.

Aiming too high—the opposite mistake—is based on over-estimating the strength of your bargaining position. People who are overconfident tend to be reluctant to make conces-sions, and as a result negotiations can often bog down and fail.[56] Indeed, in some settings taking this type of overconfi-dent approach can lead you to disaster, for mediators may perceive your demands as inflated and may rule against you.[57] Certain mediation systems, such as salary arbitration in base-ball, operate by choosing whichever position is closest to what the arbitrator estimates the true value to be. Under such an arrangement, a slight overestimate of the strength of your position can be extremely costly, because the arbitrator may rule that the other party's bid was closer to the correct value. In other situations, overestimating your position may be self-defeating because it causes you to make an overconfident bid that ends up losing to a more competitive bid by someone else.[58]

Thus, self-defeating approaches to bargaining can involve

inaccurate self-perceptions. Focusing attention one-sidedly on either your assets and strengths or on your weaknesses and vulnerabilities can produce a less-than-optimal outcome. In another kind of well-intentioned self-defeat, one that is especially familiar in the sports world, the focus of attention is again the problem. Here the self-perceptions are accurate enough, but the very focus of attention on the self results in the phenomenon known as choking, which is the subject of the next chapter.

3
Choking under Pressure

OK, let's go out and have some fun.
—Pittsburgh Steelers' coach Chuck Noll to his startled team (who were expecting a more traditional motivational speech) just before going out on the field for their first Super Bowl, which they then won convincingly

Don't be nervous, and don't make any mistakes.
—The standard words of encouragement supposedly spoken by perfectionistic dancer Fred Astaire to his partners just before a difficult scene

THE 1985 baseball season was in its final days, and all of Canada was excited over the prospect that the Toronto Blue Jays would win Canada's first division championship and, in all likelihood, go on past the league playoffs to the World Series. The season ended with a series of home games against the New York Yankees. Toronto needed to win only one more game to become the champion. Friday night was cold, but the stadium was packed as the Jays clung to a three-to-two lead in the ninth inning, just three outs away from a momentous step in Canada's sports history. The Jays' ace relief pitcher, nicknamed "the Terminator," was on the mound and in control.

One out, two outs, nobody on base. An intense hush gripped the huge crowd as the long-awaited goal came nearer: strike one, strike two. The fans were holding their breath, ready to burst forth in wild celebration. Now only one more pitch was needed. Windup, pitch, impact, and the ball went sailing over the fence for a tying home run. The crowd was stunned and so, seemingly, was the pitcher, who yielded a single and a walk to the next two batters. Suddenly the championship was no longer seconds away, and there was even a danger of the Jays losing the game.

The manager recognized that things were getting out of hand and replaced the pitcher. One of the weaker Yankee hitters was up, and by getting him out, Toronto would still preserve a good chance to win the game. The new pitcher performed effectively: he managed to get the batter to hit a soft, easy fly ball right into the air and into the glove of Toronto's center fielder, who had recently won a coveted award for flawless fielding. But, impossibly, the ball went into his glove and trickled right out onto the grass, allowing the winning run to score. The Jays had been so close, and somehow success had eluded them.

The Blue Jays had two more games and did finally manage to secure the victory needed to win the division championship. But their troubles were not over. They entered the playoffs heavily favored against a Kansas City team that really did not seem to have enough talent to win. Four victories were needed to advance to the World Series, and all of Canada was excited and hopeful. The Blue Jays easily won several early games. After the weekend games in Kansas City, the series returned to Toronto with the Jays needing only one more victory to secure the pennant and the World Series berth. It should have been easy for the Jays to win one game at home against a weaker opponent, but they seemed to fall apart once again on the brink of success. They lost the final two games in embarrassing fashion, making more fielding errors in each of those two games than they had made in the first five games combined.

Thus, Toronto did seem to have snatched defeat from the jaws of victory. Were their difficulties a fluke, an isolated episode, or a sign of some deeper character flaw in this team? None of these. Such patterns are all too familiar. The Toronto team suffered from some unusually intense pressures. Not only were they nearing the championship, but they were the center of their nation's attention, almost symbols of national pride. The championship was to be not only their first but their nation's first. And as if all of this were not disturbing enough, the team had to play its crucial game in front of thousands of its own fans who hung on every pitch and were palpably eager for the victory. This combination of factors tended to produce a level of self-consciousness that is extremely disruptive to performance and would tend to cause almost anyone to perform below capacity.

The great tennis player Arthur Ashe once pointed out, in response to questions about a recent performance by his former rival Jimmy Connors, "I don't care who you are—everybody chokes!" He was articulating a vital point about performance under pressure. Choking means failing to perform up to the best of one's ability. Pressure tends to have that effect on people in general.

Ashe's point runs contrary to the beliefs of many performers and fans. Many people find it comforting to believe that certain individuals are "chokers" who routinely fail to come through in the clutch. It is often supposed that these people suffer from some inner weakness or lack of will or psychological flaw. The reality, however, is that choking is largely a result of circumstances, not character flaws. To be sure, some people are more prone than others to choke under pressure, but these are mere differences in degree. Choking under pressure results from a reaction that is deeply rooted in the human mind. Regardless of who you are or what your character is like, you will choke sooner or later if you engage in skilled performances in various high-pressure situations. The only way to avoid choking is to be so incompetent that your performance cannot get any worse than it is already. The greater your skill, the easier it is to fall short of your capabilities on any given occasion.

Choking under pressure is a special and important kind of self-defeat. Chokers clearly bring failure on themselves, insofar as they fail or lose because they performed badly when they were capable of performing better. Yet everyone recognizes that people who choke do not want to fail; in fact, they are usually trying to do their best. Whatever changes people make when they are under pressure are intended to bring success, but instead these changes backfire and bring failure.[1] In that respect, choking resembles the backfiring strategies we covered in the last chapter. But, as we shall see, choking is not usually the result of selecting the wrong strategy because you have misjudged yourself or the world.

WHAT TURNS UP THE PRESSURE?

Choking under pressure is a vexing and perplexing problem. It can be defined as failing to perform up to capacity when it is important to do your best. Pressure can be understood simply as the importance of performing well. That is, pressure is determined by whatever is contingent on performance: If a great deal is riding on a performance, then pressure is high. If not much is riding on it, then pressure is low. Performance on any one homework assignment is not critical, so pressure is low, but the pressure rises on the final exam that may determine your course grade. Similarly, pressure is low during team practice but high during the championship game.

Pressure can also be described in terms of the size of the rewards (or punishments) that are riding on a performance. In that context, choking under pressure can be seen as a reversal of some basic psychological principles. Normally, behavior is encouraged by rewards (or avoidance of punishments) associated with that behavior. A rat will learn more quickly to press a bar or stand on its hind legs if food is dependent on its doing so. But when the rewards are linked to superior performance, sometimes people choke—that is, they perform badly precisely when the rewards are calling for good performance. For this reason, choking under pressure has been called a paradoxical incentive effect, for the incentives lead to exactly the opposite of the desired behavior.[2] Offering an incentive for good performance elicits poor performance.

That opposite reaction is also the reason we have chosen to feature choking under pressure as a form of self-defeating behavior. Somehow, people manage to do the opposite of what is in their best interests. They want to perform their best, yet they fail. Moreover, this phenomenon is not an isolated accident but a systematic pattern that can be demonstrated across a randomly chosen group of people. For example, in one experiment people were given time to learn a simple skill task and then asked to perform it as best they could. By random draw, half of them were offered a cash reward if they could match their best previous performance, while the others were given no such incentive. Ironically, the people who were offered money ended up performing worse than the ones who had nothing to gain.[3] Thus, a randomly chosen group of people systematically choked under the pressure of cash rewards.

Of course, pressure is not restricted to cash prizes. Anything that increases the importance of a particular performance can contribute to pressure.[4] If grades, chances for advancement, or other rewards are there, pressure is increased. The presence of an audience can constitute pressure, for it is more important to do well when others are watching than when you are alone. (Some audiences—such as experts, evaluators, or people you want to impress—are especially important and raise pressure that much more.) Even just being down to your last chance increases pressure, because doing well is more important. After all, if you will be allowed to try again, the importance of succeeding *this* time is reduced.

Choking under pressure can occur in an interpersonal arena as readily as in the solo performance. For example, a popular saying among salespeople is that "you can never land a deal you cannot afford to lose." The reasoning behind this insight is that by pressing too hard to close a sale that means a great deal in terms of self-esteem or financial need, you convey an aura of either desperation or insecurity—emotional states that are anathema to effective selling. On the other hand, a salesperson with an air of "Who needs you?" often attracts prospective clients. By *not* trying to influence a customer's purchasing decision, the salesperson conveys confidence and trust in the quality of the product.

Similarly, many single people are perplexed to discover that they are most attractive to the opposite sex when they are involved in steady relationships and not actively looking for romance. When out playing the field and hungering for a relationship—a situation akin to being an overinvolved salesperson—they fail to attract interest from members of the opposite sex.

HOW PEOPLE CHOKE

In choking under pressure, people somehow lose control over their own performance process. It is not that they want to fail or that they quit trying, although such reactions may occur in other contexts. As mentioned earlier, they usually want very much to succeed and are trying their best to perform well, yet somehow they cannot make themselves do what they want. Choking under pressure is thus a form of self-regulation failure. Normally, people exert considerable control over their minds and bodies. Choking under pressure is a loss of this control, an inability to make yourself do what you are normally able to do.

The fact that choking can be a loss of control over your *mind,* just as much as over your body, is important. The concept of choking under pressure is most familiar in connection with sports performances, but similar things happen with mental skills and performances. Test anxiety, for example, is a pattern of panic that sets in when you can't make your mind produce the answers that it knows. It is not a matter of ignorance or stupidity or not having studied. You may have prepared well and known the material before the test began, but faced with the exam paper, your mind goes blank.

Such reactions are not limited to tests. Consider what happened to one bright, promising ninth grader. Her English teacher told the class to memorize a speech from a Shakespeare play. Beth had an excellent memory (indeed, she later graduated at the top of her high school class and went to Cornell) and easily mastered it. The night before she was to recite it in class, she practiced the speech in her room at home and recited it half a dozen times through, flawlessly. The next day in class, she volunteered to go first. She got up in front of the class and began. But suddenly, mysteriously, the lines would not come to mind. She began to blush, groping for lines, painfully aware of the other students staring at her, the teacher listening silently. The teacher gave her a prompt and she went a couple lines further, only to become stuck again. She was embarrassed, frustrated, even humiliated. But perhaps most of all, as she said later, she was bewildered. How could she have failed? It was not that she had not prepared, for she knew the material impeccably. Somehow, though, her memory had refused to deliver the lines to her just when it was most important.

To understand how choking occurs, it is necessary to appreciate the normal operation of skills. When you begin to learn a skill, you pay conscious attention to each detail and try to learn to execute each part of the task correctly. At this stage you normally are very slow and awkward. With practice, however, the process goes increasingly smoothly and automatically. During your first piano or guitar lessons, you have to check each finger to see that it is placed correctly, and you carefully direct the fingers' awkward movements around the keyboard or fretboard. An accomplished musician no longer attends to such details, however, for the fingers have long since learned to do the job without conscious direction. An expert can simply think of what he or she wants to play, and the fingers carry out these commands. It is the same with learning to type, to use a tennis racket, or to apply other skills.[5]

Thus, a skill involves the ability to do things without thinking about them or, more precisely, without attending to the details of the process. The knowledge of how to perform becomes overlearned, automatic, and unconscious. The conscious mind is not involved in the process; in fact, it would only get in the way. Worse than unnecessary, it would be an interference.

Such interference is what causes people to choke under

pressure. The essence of choking is that the conscious mind tries to get involved in these well-learned, automatic processes that normally run smoothly without conscious interference. But the conscious mind does not contain the knowledge of how to perform effectively to maximum advantage. So when the conscious mind takes over, it merely fouls up the execution, and the performance goes badly.

Consider the example of an expert pianist. As long as her conscious mind is concentrating on the feeling expressed in Mozart's melodies or on how to interpret a particular passage or on what improvisations she wishes to make, her fingers find the keys by themselves. In contrast, if she tries to direct her fingers consciously to play all the correct keys, she is likely to find herself suddenly becoming awkward, slow, and uncertain. The more she attends to each finger movement, the more mistakes she will make (unless she slows down greatly, which ruins the performance anyway).

Why does the conscious mind suddenly intrude where it is no longer needed and is, indeed, counterproductive? The answer seems to be that this is simply a standard response to pressure. As we saw earlier, pressure is largely a matter of importance, and in particular a conscious appreciation of the importance of the performance. Because it is important to do well, you pay more attention to what you are doing. In many tasks, of course, that is a good thing, for paying more attention enables you to avoid certain kinds of careless mistakes. But paying attention to a skilled process is definitely not helpful.

Choking under pressure, then, is mediated by a shift in attention. You start paying attention to yourself, to what you are doing, and especially to *how* you are doing it. And this increased attention ends up interfering with your execution. That is why choking is often linked to experiences that increase self-consciousness, such as Beth's experience when she found herself in front of the class and unable to summon up the lines she knew by heart. With all those people staring at her, she became acutely self-conscious, and her conscious mind was unable to force her memory to yield up the appropriate contents.

Indeed, anything that increases self-consciousness before a skilled performance will tend to increase the chance of choking under pressure. This may be one reason that professional athletes tend not to acknowledge the presence of the crowd during a contest. Fans are often put off by athletes who return to the dugout or the bench without waving or showing any response to the thousands of people who are clapping so loudly for them. Yet it is dangerous for athletes to acknowledge that they are the center of so much attention, because that concentrated, focused approval might make them self-conscious and interfere with their performance a few minutes later. Indeed, professional baseball players use the expression "growing rabbit ears" to refer to the danger of becoming aware of the crowd. A player's rabbit ears, like the old-fashioned television antenna, pick up signals, and all that incoming attention tends to make him extremely self-aware and disrupts performance.

Television cameras can have similar effects. Indeed, many research studies have used television cameras expressly to make people self-aware, in order to study the psychology of self-awareness.[6] A world championship ski match in which the great Swedish skier Ingmar Stenmark was defending his title may have been a case in point. Although Stenmark was unquestionably the best in the world at the time of the tournament, other skiers had performed well and the standings were extremely close. Stenmark was one of the last to ski on the final round, and although he held the lead, he had to perform close to his best to win. As he prepared to make his run, the television cameras repeatedly focused on him, enabling the announcers to discuss the drama and the pressure—understandably, since sports events are, ultimately, entertainment. Unlike the athletes who had already finished and who therefore grinned and waved to the cameras, Stenmark kept turning away and trying to escape their intrusive gaze, but they kept following and finding him. In the end, his performance was off by just enough to cost him the championship.

Can we be certain that Stenmark choked on that occasion and that the TV cameras caused it? No. It is almost impossible to assert that any particular performance is a choke, because everyone's performance fluctuates from one occasion to another, and a poor performance could conceivably reflect simply this chance variation. It is necessary to do careful comparisons involving broad groups of performances to verify that choking occurs. Although in this chapter we use a number of individual examples to clarify and illustrate the key points about how people choke, these are merely illustrative examples. There is simply no way of determining that a particular performance by a particular person on a particular occasion was a result of choking. One can establish choking in the aggregate, but never in a particular instance. Thus, if a player always strikes out when he comes to bat with the bases loaded (but not at other times), we can conclude that he tends to choke, because there is a statistically reliable difference in his responses that occur over and over, systematically. But if he strikes out once, it is hard to be certain that he choked, because the possibility of striking out once is always there.

PRAISE, SUCCESS, HOME-TEAM SUPPORT—AND DISASTER

Several other key factors can make people self-aware and hence cause them to choke. Three that sound positive— praise, success, and fan support—can throw people off badly.

The Pressure of Praise

Compliments call attention to the recipient, and indeed many people feel self-conscious when someone pays them a compliment. Thus, ironically, you can praise people as a way of making them choke. This was illustrated by a minor incident that occurred several years ago in a National Basketball Association game between the Boston Celtics and the Cleveland Cavaliers. Late in the game, a Boston player fouled one of the rookies on the Cleveland squad, who prepared to go to the line for some fairly important foul shots. During the TV timeout, one of the older members of the Boston team went up to the Cleveland rookie and complimented him on having had a fine season and having done so well in his first year. The Cleveland player was surprised and very gratified to receive such praise from a famous, established star. Then he went to the line and missed both foul shots. "There's a rookie for you," said the Boston player, loudly enough for everyone to hear. Apparently, his praise had been disingenuous; he knew that it was an effective means of making someone choke.

Again, we cannot be absolutely certain that the Cavaliers rookie choked, for occasionally players do miss both foul shots in the natural course of shooting. But it does appear that the Boston veteran believed that praise can cause choking, because he deliberately timed his praise to disrupt the players' execution. Moreover, laboratory studies have shown that compliments do cause people to choke. One series of studies showed that a well-timed compliment can cause people's performance to drop systematically, as compared with that of other people who received no compliment at the same time.[7] In fact, the most effective ploy is to compliment someone on some attribute unrelated to the performance, because a relevant compliment can occasionally boost confidence and thereby help performance. In those studies, people who were complimented for their hairstyle or clothing were most prone to choke on a video-skill task performance, although many people choked after being complimented on their video skills as well. Praise for your hairstyle makes you self-conscious without boosting your confidence, so its effects on task performance are most systematically harmful.

The Burden of Success

Another important factor that induces choking is the prospect of fulfilling your dream and becoming a major champion (or other successful person), especially for the first time. Interestingly, the occurrence of reaching a goal is one of the more widely accepted psychoanalytic explanations for self-defeat, although our analysis of why people hit bottom once they reach the top is radically different from that put forth by most psychodynamically oriented theorists.[8] Freud's clinical practice led him to the conclusion that "people occasionally fall ill precisely because a deeply rooted and long-cherished wish has come to fulfillment,"[9] evoking a sense of guilt that prevents them from enjoying success. Some psychoanalysts have also argued that people fear success. Some theorists propose that the performance pressures implied in goal attainment drive people to self-destruct when they are on the verge of obtaining success.

The psychoanalyst Karen Horney was among the first to note that psychoanalytic patients often sabotage therapy the moment their analyst conveys favorable feedback or suggests that their treatment may be moving toward a successful resolution.[10] These so-called negative therapeutic reactions were thought to derive from patients' fears that if they attained success they would be subjected to both performance pressures and social censure from people who might envy their progress or be jealous of their newly achieved status. The recognition that these interpersonal pressures could motivate self-sabotage represents a rare deviation within the psychoanalytic community from traditional perspectives on self-destructive outcomes.

Modern analyses of the stresses inherent in success lend support to this notion.[11] Grade school children who attain academic success know how ambivalent that outcome can be. Although straight-A students will be amply praised and rewarded by teachers and parents, they may suffer at the hands of classmates. To relieve the adverse consequences of sticking out from the crowd, many children sabotage their classroom performance and function as academic underachievers. Similarly, work-related promotions that advance people to the top of the corporate ladder can often cost those achievers their physical health. While this type of downside risk is rarely noticed or discussed among fast-track careerists, research has shown that career success can cause coronary heart disease as well as alcoholism.[12]

When people actualize the identities they have desired, they become very aware of themselves, especially if they are being watched by people who like them or love them.[13] Someone who has struggled for years to complete a college degree and finally goes up on stage to receive his or her diploma, with family and friends watching, is likely to become extremely self-aware. The same holds true for any other such moment: receiving a major award, being officially given an important job or promotion, or being pronounced the winner of some election or major competition. These longed-for transformations of identity are events whose fundamental meaning is the change in the definition of the self, and they almost inevitably draw attention to the self. Again, this effect is multiplied if there is an appreciative or supportive audience.

Such increased self-awareness may intensify your pleasure, but it may also cause choking if skilled performance is involved. This could become a problem for athletes who are close to winning a major championship. As they zero in on this major triumph, especially if they are playing at home in front of their fans, they may become increasingly self-aware and thus increasingly likely to choke.

The Home-Field Disadvantage

These considerations lead to a rather startling prediction: the home field may become a disadvantage when you are on the brink of a championship. Normally, of course, home teams fare better than visiting teams. Yet this home-field advantage might well disappear and even reverse when one reaches the brink of the championship.

To test this hypothesis, two researchers examined the records of over half a century of World Series games. They started with the year 1926, because that was when the World Series rules and procedures stabilized into the modern form and when the last scandalous allegations of players deliberately losing games were over. They counted every year up until the most recent season, which was then 1982. They wanted to see, simply, if home teams tended to choke in the final game of the series.[14] Among the early games of the World Series, the usual home-field advantage was found: home teams won about 60 percent of the time. But in the final game, this advantage disappeared, and home teams *lost* about 60 percent of the time. Thus, it appeared that home teams indeed fared worse when the championship was on the line than when they played in earlier games against the same opponent.

Of course, this finding was not entirely conclusive. After all, maybe the home teams were not choking—maybe, instead, the visiting teams were doing better. In baseball it is hard to know whether a particular outcome is due to good play on one side or bad play on the other. A low number of hits or runs, for example, might mean that the batters were choking, but it could also mean that the opposing pitchers were pitching well. The researchers did manage to isolate one statistic that is immune to those ambiguities, namely, the rate of fielding errors. If the shortstop drops the ball, it is not because the batter hit it especially well; indeed, it is nearly impossible to bat in a way that causes fielding errors. So they tallied up all the fielding errors in all those World Series games. Visiting teams did not change their rate of fielding errors from the early games to the final games, but the home teams approximately doubled their rate of fielding errors when it came to the final game. Thus, it seems that home teams were performing worse in the final games, rather than that visiting teams were performing better.

Note that the prospect of winning, not of losing, apparently produces this effect. After all, only winning produces the desired identity change and the resultant surge of self-awareness. It was only when the home team had a chance of becoming champions (such as when they had won three and lost two) that they lost the game. If they were behind and in danger of elimination, they performed well and usually won the game. The home fans appear to help an underdog; they are mainly disruptive to a team on the verge of winning.

Other studies have also shown that winning, not losing, is the possibility that makes people choke.[15] In a careful and detailed study researchers followed professional golfers trying to make a putt. Over and over, the pros did worse when trying for a birdie (a successful score) than when trying for par (a standard or average score).[16] Dave Pelz, who is both a teaching pro golfer and a researcher, explained the discrepancy as due to "the pressure of success" and added, "If every putt the PGA tour had measured [in this research project] had been to win the U.S. Open, my guess is that the percentages might be down another 10 percent or 20 percent."[17]

Thus, the psychological power of self-awareness produced by claiming a desired identity is crucial in causing people to choke, and this factor helps explain the difficulties encountered by the Toronto team as described at the beginning of this chapter. Trying to win a championship is hard enough, and it causes many excellent athletes to choke. The Toronto team had the added burden of trying to win not only their first championship but also their nation's first championship. They were acutely aware of the intense national attention focused on them, and it is hard to imagine that anyone could be unaffected by that high level of pressure and attention.

In some sports, the home field in the playoffs is awarded to the team with the better season record, which means it is probably the better team. In football, for example, television commentators often point out that home teams seem to fare better in the playoffs, but this fact may have nothing to do with playing at home—more likely it is because the home team is simply the better team. The National Basketball Association also assigns a home-field advantage to the team with the better record, but the tendency for home teams to choke in the final game remains. A survey of the outcomes of NBA conference and league championship series from 1967 to 1982 revealed such a pattern.[18] Home teams have an advantage in the early games, winning about 70 percent of them, but in the final game, 50 percent. Obviously, 50 percent means that they win as often as they lose, but that represents a significant drop from their normal rate of success.

ARE CHOKERS AND QUITTERS THE SAME?

An important question is whether teams (or individuals) sometimes choke because they give up. The answer is no: choking under pressure is not a reduction in effort but a failure of skill.

The distinction between effort and skill is extremely important for understanding performance and, indeed, for predicting how people will respond to pressure. Unlike skill, effort *can* be controlled by the conscious mind, so when pressure is high, self-awareness might make people do better on tasks that depend mainly on effort.

There is now considerable evidence that effort and skill follow different principles and respond very differently to external influences. In particular, pressure improves effort even though it impairs skill. A chance to win money will generally make people try harder; so if success depends simply on how hard they are trying, their performance will improve. Muscular exertion, persistence, determined concentration, and other such processes can apparently be improved by an act of will. The intrusion of consciousness therefore improves how you do. Only on skill tasks is consciousness harmful.

A useful illustration of this effect can perhaps be seen in examining soccer, which has a genuine world championship tournament involving professional teams from all over the globe. But home teams have generally done extremely well during the World Cup soccer matches, and the number of times the home team has emerged as the world champion is far above what the odds would predict.

The advantage of the home teams in soccer might well be due to jet lag or language difficulties or some other factor. Most likely, however, the advantage lies in the fact that home audiences increase effort. Physical exertion is far more important in soccer than in baseball, for example. Baseball depends mainly on finely honed skills, and it is possible to be a top baseball player without being in superb physical condition. Baseball players run for only short stretches at a time, and many things they do require neither strength nor stamina. In contrast, professional soccer players must generally run at moderate to high speeds almost continuously for ninety minutes with only one halftime break. The World Cup tournament is particularly grueling, for it requires players to perform at this strenuous level every second or third day for several weeks. By the end of the tournament, the surviving teams are physically depleted, and only excellent conditioning can prevent them from succumbing to exhaustion. In that context, a little extra adrenaline rush—stimulated occasionally by the home audience of thousands of enthusiastic fans —may make the difference between victory and defeat.

Of course, this is not to say that skill is irrelevant to soccer, for there are indeed great skills involved. But differences in skill may be small compared with differences in exertion. The point is simply that the role of effort, relative to skill, is much more decisive in soccer than in baseball or various other sports.

Accordingly, pressure and home audiences may benefit soccer teams, even though they may impair baseball teams.

The discrepancy between skill and effort may also be relevant to American football. Conventional wisdom holds that offense sells tickets but defense wins championships, and indeed many teams seem to have enjoyed great success in playoffs and Super Bowls without having an outstanding offense—as long as their defense was strong. In contrast, teams with exceptional offenses but weak defenses (such as the San Diego Chargers during the late 1970s and early 1980s) have been far less successful in the pressure-packed games leading to the Super Bowl trophy, even though they seem to have performed quite well during the season.

Why is defense more important than offense in the playoffs? One likely answer is in the skill-to-effort ratio. Defense depends more on effort and less on skill than does offense. A football offense requires elaborate coordination and remarkable feats of skill, such as are required in completing a long forward pass. Defense, in contrast, reacts to offense and depends on strength, stamina, and power. It is revealing that people often become concerned late in football games about whether the defense is being exhausted, not the offense. Announcers will say about the defense—but never the offense—"They have been out there a long time; they are probably getting tired." Again, this is not to say that there is no skill involved in defense; the point is only that effort plays a greater part than skill on defense, as compared with offense.

If offense depends on skill for success, however, then the pressure of playoff games is likely to cause the offense to choke. In the big games, players become self-conscious as their minds try to take over and direct their actions, so their performance may suffer as they put in too much effort and, for example, overthrow passes. Defense, however, is less prone to choke because skill plays a smaller role. Indeed, the added pressure and self-attention may cause defensive players to perform better than usual in the important games—and that may be why defense wins championships.

PERSONALITY AND PRESSURE

Let us turn now to the issue of personality differences. Choking is caused by attending to ourselves at key moments. That is, pressure increases our tendency to monitor every detail of our performance process, with disruptive consequences. Some people are more vulnerable than others to this effect of pressure. Researchers have developed effective tests for distinguishing between people who attend to themselves often as opposed to people who are characteristically low in self-consciousness. Perhaps ironically, the people who are normally low in self-consciousness are most prone to choke. Study after study has confirmed that choking effects are strongest and most reliable among these people.[19]

One key reason may be that people who are highly self-conscious most of the time gradually become accustomed to this state and learn to cope with it. Pressure simply puts them into a very familiar state (of being self-aware). In contrast, people who are unaccustomed to paying attention to themselves suffer the impact of pressure more. When pressure makes them self-conscious, they do not know how to handle their self-awareness, and their performance is affected more strongly.

Adolescence: A Turning Point

Some support for the notion that people learn to handle self-consciousness can be derived by examining developmental patterns in performing under pressure. As many experts have noted, self-consciousness increases markedly during adolescence. Before adolescence, children do not have that keen sensitivity to how others see them.

In one study researchers examined people's performance under pressure as a function of age.[20] In this experiment people performed popular video games alone and then again with someone watching them. By comparing the performance in isolation against the pressured audience performance, the researchers could see broad patterns in choking. Apparently, many younger (preadolescent) children did not become awkward and self-conscious simply because someone was watching them. In fact, up to the age of twelve, children performed better when there was an audience than when they were alone. But all of this changed abruptly at adolescence. Teenagers in general choked badly when they had an audience. Adults over age twenty showed some tendency to choke, but it was not as strong or as uniform as that of the teenagers.

The implication is that the capacity for self-consciousness increases greatly around the onset of adolescence. The pressure of having an audience is most disruptive to teenagers because they are fully sensitive to it but have not yet learned to handle it. As they grow older, they are still fully able to see themselves from another's viewpoint, but some adults learn strategies for coping with self-consciousness.

Choke-Prone or Choke-Proof?

Could people become immune to choking by maintaining a very low level of self-consciousness? There is some evidence that this is so. Using some new personality measurement techniques, researchers have sorted people not just by how much self-awareness they typically feel but also by how much they fluctuate.[21] A wide cross section of these people were then tested on performance under pressure. Several clear distinctions between choke-prone and choke-proof personalities emerged.

The choke-prone personality is characteristic of people who typically pay minimal attention to themselves but do occasionally feel very self-conscious. Such people usually do not reflect on their own actions, wonder how they seem to others, or spend a lot of time in introspection. But they do have the capacity to become highly aware of themselves, and occasional situations elicit that reaction from them. These people showed the largest and most consistent tendency to choke under pressure. Thus, the choke-prone personality is characterized by low but unstable levels of self-attention.

In contrast, the choke-proof personality is characteristic of people whose attention to themselves is *consistently* low. These people do not reflect on their own actions, wonder how others see them, introspect, or pay much attention to themselves in other ways. In this respect they are quite similar to the choke-prone people. The difference is that they do not exhibit that vulnerability to becoming highly self-aware in a few situations. These people showed the least tendency to choke under pressure. The choke-proof personality is characterized by low and stable levels of self-attention.

In between the choke-prone and choke-proof individuals were the people who are often self-conscious and are apparently familiar with the state of attending to themselves. Pressure does not seem to alter their state greatly; or if it does affect them, they have already learned ways of dealing with this state in order to perform effectively. After all, if you are self-conscious most of the time, you are likely to learn to function while self-conscious.

At present, then, the best conclusion about personality

and choking under pressure is that choking results when pressure puts you into a highly unfamiliar state of self-awareness. If you do not become self-conscious under any circumstances, then you are not likely to choke under pressure. And if the self-focused state is familiar, then you are not greatly handicapped by it.

Still, we should point out again that when the situation is sufficiently compelling, it will affect almost anyone, regardless of personality. For us, a convincing demonstration of this fact concerned the great tennis champion Martina Navratilova, who proved over many years that she was as capable as any athlete anywhere of performing superbly under enormous pressure. Yet even she could be affected if the conditions were strong enough, as happened at the 1984 French Open when she was trying to complete the grand slam.

The grand slam is the highest possible achievement in tennis. It entails winning the four biggest tournaments in the same year. Because no one had achieved this in many, many years, the rules were revised slightly in 1982 so that the grand-slam award would be given to anyone who won the four tournaments consecutively within a year's time, even if they did not all take place in the same calendar year. Navratilova was at the height of her skill when this rule change was made, and she seized the opportunity. She won Wimbledon in July 1983, then the U.S. Open, then the Australian Open. All that remained was the French Open.

At the French, she was fully in control; no other woman could match her. She dominated her early opponents and reached the finals. Even there, against her greatest rival, she won the first set fairly easily and became invincible in the second. Her opponent could scarcely win a point off Navratilova's serve, and Navratilova headed fiercely toward sweeping the set, which would have placed her in tennis history as only the third woman ever to win a grand slam. She won five games without losing any and was only two points away from winning the match when abruptly, mysteriously, her skill seemed to desert her. She lost a series of points, lost the game, and lost the next game as well. Fortunately for her, she did recover to win the set and match. Still, that brief period of diminished skill was an odd blemish on an otherwise dominating performance, and it is probably no accident that it occurred just when she was about to enlarge her place in tennis history significantly.

Thus, even an experienced, proven, and seemingly unflappable champion could apparently become self-conscious when the conditions were strong enough. In this case, she was about to become the third woman ever to reach that plateau of achievement that would guarantee her a prominent place in the century-old history of her sport. The full meaning of such an event for one's identity cannot help but make one self-conscious, and the skills of even an accomplished veteran cannot entirely resist the onslaught of such a mental shift.

From well-intentioned styles of self-defeating behavior, in which people unwittingly cause themselves suffering without any mitigating gains, we now turn to styles of self-defeat in which they receive something in return for their pain. In the chapter that follows, we look at some of the factors that affect the choices people make in weighing the potential costs or risks of their behavior against the benefits they might reap.

4

Trade-offs: Taking the Bad along with the Good

We had to destroy the town in order to save it.
—American officer explaining the destruction of a Vietnamese village

GARY, an insurance agent, had lived his life the way he wanted.[1] He was not an alcoholic, but he enjoyed his martinis. Each day he smoked several cigars as well as half a pack of cigarettes. He ate whatever he wanted, including sweet desserts and high-fat meats. He never exercised. With two grown, successful sons, a good marriage, and a successful business career, Gary was a happy man.

In his early fifties, Gary had a heart attack. His physician told him that he needed to change his lifestyle drastically. He was overweight, with high blood pressure and a weak heart. If he wanted to live to see his grandchildren, he would have to quit smoking and drinking, start a mild exercise regimen such as taking walks, and change his diet drastically.

Gary made some changes but soon went back to his old lifestyle. Life was simply no fun without all the small pleasures he had come to depend on. Within three months he had given up the evening walks and had gone back to his martinis and cigars. He told himself that he had cut down a little and that he would take his chances. Two years later, a second heart attack killed him.

Were Gary's actions self-destructive? He was told how to change his lifestyle in order to live longer, but he ignored this advice and the healthy patterns he needed. Sure enough, he died young, just as his physician had predicted. Although we can't be certain about any single case, it definitely appears that Gary destroyed himself.

But Gary's actions were not motivated by any desire to die. He enjoyed his lifestyle—unhealthy habits and all. He went back to smoking and drinking simply because he liked those things too much to give them up. His death was not a disguised form of suicide, not a deliberate act of self-destruction. With pleasure came risks. He could have given up his pleasures and reduced the danger, or he could have had his pleasures along with their risks. He accepted the risk, and so he died.

Gary provides a good illustration of an important category of self-defeating behavior. People make choices that bring them both good and bad results. In making choices, they accept—outright or implicitly—some undesirable results such as risks or costs, trading those off against the benefits and advantages. Each decision is a trade-off. There are no perfect or ideal choices, and self-defeating ones are far from ideal.

A trade-off is thus a kind of bargain, in which one chooses some course of action that has both costs and rewards. To be sure, many actions involve both costs and rewards, and the mere presence of some costs hardly qualifies a choice as self-destructive—otherwise, nearly all decisions or actions would contain some element of self-defeat. Self-destruction is involved, however, when you make a bad bargain, that is, when the costs outweigh the benefits, as they certainly did in Gary's case. Often it is difficult to know at the time whether you are making a good or bad bargain, and sometimes weighing the balance of costs and rewards is subjective even in retrospect. In some instances a self-defeatist may eventually agree that he or she made a bad choice—that is, one with benefits that were not worth the costs or risks. The question is, Did that self-defeatist intend to strike a bad bargain?

Knowingly Taking Risks

Let's consider three possible levels of intention in self-defeating behavior.[2] At one extreme, the self-defeatist might want to suffer and would therefore deliberately select a course of action to bring on that suffering. Thus, in deliberate self-defeat, suffering would be both foreseen and desired. The opposite extreme is the case in which the self-defeatist does not at all want to suffer or fail and instead holds very positive, rational, comprehensible goals—but unfortunately chooses a course of action that brings about the opposite of what he or she wanted or intended. These backfiring strategies have already been covered in the last two chapters. In between those two extremes are the trade-offs, in which the self-defeatist, like Gary, accepts risks and costs as a necessary accompaniment of some appealing benefit he or she chooses. In trade-offs, the harm to yourself is foreseeable but not desired.

Obviously, if the costs are small and the rewards large, it seems more appropriate to speak of the trade-off as a good bargain rather than as self-defeating behavior. It is only self-defeating if the costs outweigh the benefits in some respect, such as in your own retrospective view.

Still, the calculation of costs and benefits is complicated because many behaviors involve immediate benefits but delayed risks or harm. For example, smoking cigarettes brings immediate pleasure but increases the long-term risks for lung cancer or emphysema. The calculation is further complicated because we often can talk only of probable risks and the chances for harm. Many people smoke cigarettes for years without getting cancer. Whether or not they get cancer will probably be a major factor in determining whether they decide, in retrospect, that smoking was a self-destructive pattern or a good pastime. Several times a day Gary felt a desire to smoke a cigar. Each small decision offered one fairly certain outcome—namely, the guaranteed pleasure of the smoke—and one highly uncertain one—namely, the risk that this smoking would eventually harm him. When he was younger, before his first heart attack, the danger must have seemed even more remote and the immediate pleasure even more enjoyable.

With some trade-offs, then, people obviously end up doing themselves more harm than good. These cases clearly constitute self-defeating behavior. Let us examine some of them. There is a clear pattern. First, potential exists for benefits as well as harm and costs, so the self-defeating outcomes are typically an unwanted by-product of the quest for some benefit. Second, the benefits tend to be immediate, whereas the costs tend to be delayed, often well into the future. Third, the benefits tend to be guaranteed, whereas the costs may take the form of possible risks.

SUBSTANCE ABUSE

One well-known self-destructive trade-off involves substance abuse.[3] Alcohol, tobacco, and many mind-altering drugs have been shown to harm personal health. Like Gary, most users are aware of these effects, yet they use the substances anyway, often to excess. Drinking, smoking, and taking mind-altering drugs thus are potentially self-destructive, and the harm to oneself is at least foreseeable. Indeed, every package of cigarettes contains an explicit warning about these dangers, so it would be hard to avoid realizing that smoking is harmful.

Why do people smoke tobacco, take drugs, or drink alcohol? There are many reasons, one of which (self-handicapping) is covered in the next chapter. But a main reason is that it makes people feel good. The consumption of alcohol or other drugs produces pleasant sensations.

Among habitual users, pleasure is intensified by the appeasement of addictive cravings, as shown in research that examined cigarette smokers' claims about smoking as an important way to relax.[4] This claim is paradoxical, because nicotine is a stimulant, so it should cause arousal, not relaxation. The physiological truth is that someone who smokes a cigarette or otherwise ingests nicotine will experience arousal. But once people become addicted to nicotine, they depend on regular doses of it. If deprived of nicotine, even for a fairly short time (perhaps a matter of hours, or in some cases even less), they go into addictive withdrawal, which produces another form of arousal. Having a cigarette will end the withdrawal state: this *feels* like relaxation. So a regular smoker who has a cigarette is not relaxed in comparison with a nonsmoker; the cigarette doesn't bring relaxation beyond normal levels. But that smoker will be relaxed in comparison with another regular smoker who has not had a cigarette recently and is therefore experiencing withdrawal.

Thus, taking these substances makes people feel good. A second benefit is that they help people escape from an awareness of themselves. The need to blot out unpleasant, troublesome, or depressing self-focused thoughts about oneself underlies a broad assortment of human actions, ranging from spiritual striving to masochism to suicide.[5] Some of these efforts to get rid of self-awareness have destructive effects on

the self, and substance abuse is a clear example of these destructive side effects. Alcohol reduces self-awareness,[6] and
smoking may do the same. For example, nervous people find
that smoking gives them something to do with their hands, and
the preoccupation with smoking activities can help take their
minds off their worries about looking bad or feeling stupid.[7]
Less is known about illegal drugs (because the illegality makes
it much harder for scientists to conduct research with them),
but some of them probably have similar effects. Thus, substance abuse is a form of self-destructive behavior motivated
by people's desire to avoid thinking badly of themselves.

Substance abuse fits the pattern of self-defeating trade-offs
in two further respects. First, its benefits are immediate,
whereas its costs become apparent only later. Having a few
drinks makes you feel good right away, but the hangover
doesn't come until morning, and the liver damage or the
disruption of your career and marriage may not become apparent for years. Similarly, smoking cigarettes or using heroin
offers immediate pleasure, but the costs and problems come
only after months or even years. Thus, substance abuse seems
to fit the pattern of accepting long-term costs and risks to gain
immediate satisfactions.

Second, the benefits of substance abuse are fairly certain,
while the costs are often a matter of probabilities. Smoking
does not guarantee that you'll get cancer or emphysema. Indeed, your life might be ended next year by a car crash or a
nuclear war, and then it would not make any difference
whether you had smoked or not. Meanwhile, the pleasure of
smoking a cigarette or having a drink is something you can
count on experiencing every time. Again, then, we see the
pattern of uncertain or delayed self-destructive outcomes
versus clearcut or immediate benefits. People seem more
willing to choose a sure thing than to take a chance, even

when the former may be quite trivial compared with the latter.

The very uncertainty of the harmful outcomes (such as an early death from lung cancer) makes evaluating the rationality of the decision complex. If smoking cigarettes or snorting cocaine were guaranteed to shorten lives, then it might be safe to label those decisions as bad. But many smokers and drug users die of other causes.

PROCRASTINATION

Procrastination is an important and familiar category of self-defeat that is just now catching researchers' attention.[8] Many people put things off until the last minute; but when the last minute arrives, they find that they cannot get the job done well in so little time. Postponing the project thus turns into a mechanism of self-defeat, because they cause themselves anguish and stress and possibly failure.

Procrastination must be understood as a trade-off. People do not set out to put themselves in a desperate, stressful situation. Rather, each day when they could be working on some project, they find something else they would rather do. This series of small, casual decisions gradually puts them into a desperate situation marked by a looming deadline. Procrastination can be a form of self-handicapping, another form of self-defeating trade-off, which we discuss in chapter 5.

What are the benefits of procrastination? There are several answers. An easy and obvious one is that it is more fun to relax or play than to work on something difficult, so each day tough jobs get put off. This answer, though undoubtedly correct in some cases, is not the only explanation. In fact, some procrastinators work very hard at other things, so they cannot be accused of relaxing or enjoying themselves instead of working. Many of our acquaintances have told us how they avoid working at some task by finding other useful things to do, such as cleaning the apartment or waxing the car.

Procrastination is sometimes linked to anxieties and insecurities: people postpone working on things that bring up threatening worries about their competence. The feeling that "only my best will do" is one basis for the form of procrastination known to motivate self-handicapping strategies. As we explain in chapter 5, people often put off starting a task when the implications of failure are directly linked to their self-image. Some cases of writer's block fall in this category. Writers sometimes find themselves unable to make progress on the book or article they are writing, especially when there is some demand that the book or article be extremely good. Each time they sit down to write, they only come up with work that is less than the best, and the pressure to be superb becomes so daunting that they end up with an anxiety attack instead of a rough draft. In such cases, we can readily understand why they might suddenly remember that the kitchen floor needs to be washed and waxed. As long as they are moving the mop around the kitchen floor, they have a good excuse for not making progress with the writing, and such mundane tasks can even be satisfying because progress is so palpable. When they are finished, they have a clean and beautiful floor to show for their efforts. In contrast, a day spent writing page after page only to tear those all up leaves them with nothing.

Procrastination has added advantages if you are beset with such anxieties. The pressure to excel may be so intimidating that you cannot accept anything you produce because it is not good enough. After you have procrastinated, however, and the deadline approaches, suddenly it is too late to worry about being terrific. You have to have something to turn in, and so you just do the best that is possible in the short time remaining. In other words, procrastination removes the pressure for excellence.[9] This analysis might seem quixotic, because time pressure replaces pressure for quality performance, which may be the overriding problem. For many people, it is not difficult to produce something merely adequate, but it is difficult and distressing to have to produce something superb. In fact, producing something adequate at the last minute may even feel like a triumph.

Consider the case of Celia. She had a major report due in several months, and she had some reason to believe that if the report turned out to be excellent, her career would take off. At first she had a seemingly perfect reason not to work on the report: she did not yet have all the necessary information. Her other, regular duties were keeping her plenty busy, so she simply put off thinking about the report. She stacked the first materials for the report together on a shelf and told herself she would tackle that later, when everything else was ready. The data for the report came to her in small chunks, and gradually, almost imperceptibly, she passed the point where she did have enough to begin work, and then the point where she had everything she needed. But she continued to leave the stack untouched on the shelf while she focused on her other duties.

The stack stopped growing, and the deadline began to creep up. When her boss asked her how the report was coming, she felt a moment of anxious concern, but she answered with a bright smile that she had just about all the information she needed and was almost ready to start writing. Her boss gave her a friendly reminder of how important the report was and how much it could do for her, but instead of reassuring her, this made her feel nervous and worried. She worked harder than usual on her day-to-day tasks.

As the deadline drew closer, she forced herself to take the

stack off the shelf on several occasions. She sorted and orga-
nized the information and fretted about the best way to get
started. But then would come a phone call or other distraction,
and she would put the material back on the shelf and attend
to other things. Although she would always make some gesture
of annoyance or frustration, she secretly felt relieved. Meanwhile, when anyone asked, she could honestly say that she had
been working on the report, that it was coming along, and that
it would be ready in time.

When she had first received the assignment to write the
report, she had been flattered and excited, especially because
of the possibility that her career would benefit. By this point,
however, those positive feelings were gone. She was intimi-
dated by the pressure to make the report superb, and she had
begun to worry about what would happen if it flopped. She
had shared her initial excitement with her husband, Bob, but
now she felt that his support and encouragement were further
burdens to her. If she failed to turn out a stellar report, she
would be letting him down, too. Occasionally he asked her
how the report was coming, and she felt he was pressuring her,
undermining her. Her brittle replies soon discouraged him
from mentioning it. Meanwhile, she continued to recalculate
how long it would actually take her to write the report, concluding each time that she didn't absolutely have to start today,
that there was still enough time for her to get it done.

Celia's procrastination had a predictable outcome. She
failed to start working on the report in earnest until the
deadline was almost upon her. She had left herself barely
enough time to get it done, by her own calculations; but
because she had underestimated how long the job would
take (which people routinely do), she found there was simply
not enough time. It emerged that she did not have a couple
of necessary pieces of information after all, so the project

was held up while she collected them. She went to her boss and asked for an extension on the deadline, citing the missing information as a source of unanticipated delay. Her boss agreed but was clearly displeased. By now she had stopped thinking of the report as a way of boosting her career; she was simply trying to ward off disaster. She was able to turn in a report by the second deadline, although she had not washed her hair, eaten a proper meal, or had a decent night's sleep for almost a week. The report was adequate but definitely not a masterpiece, and the hoped-for promotion did not ensue. Still, when she turned in the report, she felt both relief and a distinct sense of pride at having gotten it done at all. She and her husband even had a small celebration, despite her having blown a fine career opportunity.

DISOBEYING THE DOCTOR

Another form of self-defeating trade-offs can be found in health psychology, or more specifically in the way people respond to treatments and medicines their physicians recommend. Doctors have long suspected that many patients fail to take all their medicine as prescribed, to get the full recommended rest, and to follow other medical recommendations. Recent studies have confirmed a startling disregard for professional care and advice. Across different studies, rates for compliance with the doctor's orders have ranged from a high of 82 percent (which is still only four out of five patients) down to a low of 20 percent.[10] People keep only about 75 percent of the medical appointments they make, and when someone else (such as a spouse or parent) makes the appointment, the no-show rate is around half. Likewise, about half of all patients fail to comply with their long-term treatment programs.[11]

Why Not Take the Doctor's Advice?

A number of factors have been shown to affect compliance rates. An important one is the frequency and severity of patients' symptoms. People generally comply well with treatments that provide relief from painful, annoying, or disruptive symptoms. Patients who see their symptoms as intolerable will seek treatment and generally follow it. When symptoms are not so bothersome, however, people comply much less, even if the disease is severe.[12]

So from a behavioral standpoint, the diseases that *don't* make people feel sick are the most dangerous, because people with those illnesses are most likely to neglect taking their medicine and following the doctor's orders. Much the same happens when a prescribed medicine quickly clears up the symptoms of an illness but only later resolves the underlying problem. People will take the medicine until they feel better and then stop. They are not cured, and the problem will come back. In fact, people sometimes have symptoms wholly unrelated to their disease, yet they discontinue treatment once the symptoms disappear—a very dangerous pattern in dealing with a serious disease.

Another factor is the unpleasantness of the treatment itself. Some treatments are painful or otherwise uncomfortable, and people are much more likely to fail to comply with those. Dental care provides a good example. Most people value their teeth, and they realize that professional dental care is best for them. But they associate going to the dentist with pain and discomfort—drilling, clamping, vibrating, and simply having another person's fingers in their mouth—and avoid such visits as long as possible.

Even if the treatment is not painful, people may avoid it because of the cost in time and money. People comply less with expensive treatments than with affordable ones. Likewise, they comply less with time-consuming treatments than with quicker ones. Even chronically ill patients are less likely to show up for appointments that interfere with their daily routines than for more convenient treatments.[13]

Enjoy Today, Pay Tomorrow

In short, many people routinely disregard expert advice from their physicians and fail to comply with their treatments. These failures can literally be self-destructive, because serious damage to health can result. The reasons for these failures conform to the patterns we have already seen. People choose short-term, immediate benefits over long-term risks or costs. Noncompliance with medical care often arises from a desire to avoid immediate pain and discomfort, to avoid inconvenience, or to save time or money. When the short-term rewards are high—such as getting immediate relief from pain or bothersome symptoms—people comply very well. But when the short-term yield is neutral or aversive (as in painful treatments), people are more likely not to comply. They accept the long-term dangers for the sake of the short-term relief, freedom, or security.

Likewise, in many cases people accept an increased long-term risk to get a more certain immediate result. Eating salty or high-cholesterol foods or drinking alcohol—even if prohibited by a physician—will almost certainly yield some immediate pleasure. The negative side of disobeying such orders is an increased chance of serious illness or death. As in the previous examples of trade-offs, people seem to disregard the uncertain outcomes, even if these *could* be severe.

A chilling illustration of this disregard has been provided in recent studies about skin cancer. Early in this century, people in the fashionably white-skinned upper classes wanted to avoid suntans, because sun-browned skin was common among Caucasian manual laborers. The increased fashionability of tennis and other outdoor sports, however, along with other factors, reversed this preference so that by the 1950s affluent whites wanted a deep tan. In the 1970s growing evidence revealed the dangers associated with tanning, especially skin cancer, which can be fatal. Still, you can walk along almost any beach in hot weather and see people lying in the sun trying to alter their bodies' color despite the risks.

The wish for a tan is not too surprising. People's willingness to accept small and distant risks for the sake of certain and short-term gains has been demonstrated over and over in this chapter's review of self-defeating trade-offs. What is more surprising is that many people apparently fail to learn even when they have a brush with a deadly disease. In a recent study of 1,000 people who had had surgery for skin cancer, the researchers found that over one-third of the patients still failed to use a sunscreen, and one-fourth of them had gone back to full-fledged sunbathing. The trade-off was identified by one physician, who summarized the attitude of these people (mostly women) by saying, "Skin cancer was not enough of a problem to give up a tan."[14] For these people, taking the risk seems especially foolish, because of their increased chances for a recurrence. Even if the skin cancer is not fatal, its effect on their appearance may well outweigh whatever attractiveness is gained by tanning. As with many other self-defeating trade-offs, those who want only to enjoy today may eventually pay heavy prices for their choices.

THE PRICE OF SAVING FACE

Let us turn now to a form of self-defeating behavior that arises in the context of embarrassment and desires for revenge. Revenge comes in many shapes and sizes, and chapter 6 focuses on Pyrrhic revenge. But for now we are discussing revenge in a more general fashion.

A pervasive human motive is to avoid looking bad. People hate to lose face. When something threatens to make them look bad, they become very upset and go to some lengths to prevent the loss of face or to repair the damage to their image. They will accept substantial costs to accomplish these ends, and sometimes these costs can be large enough to make the response seem irrational, foolish, and even self-defeating.

The first goal is to stop whatever is causing the loss of face. People will accept tangible, even financial, losses to bring an embarrassing situation to an immediate close. For example, in certain research studies, subjects were falsely told that the study involved analyzing voice patterns, which served as a pretext for making a tape recording of each subject's voice.[15] The subjects were then asked to sing a corny and embarrassing song such as "Love Is a Many Splendored Thing," without accompaniment, while a researcher pretended to observe them and record them. The subjects were told that what they would be paid depended on how much data they furnished—which meant how long they sang. Thus, they had a financial incentive to sing slowly and drag out the song. Instead of doing that, however, many subjects sang as rapidly as possible, in order to end the embarrassing situation. Whether these trade-offs are a good or a bad bargain may be difficult to establish, but it is nonetheless surprising that people will abandon their primary goals (in the subjects' case, acquiring money) and sacrifice gain to avoid a temporary feeling of embarrassment.

The existence of the United States as an independent nation may be traced in part to this sort of self-defeating behavior. The British provoked the Revolutionary War largely because of concerns over face—revenge for humiliation. As the conflicts with the American colonists escalated, some British experts convincingly calculated that there was nothing to gain by using force. Indeed, they knew that even if they *won* the war, they would end up losing, because no benefit of winning a war with the American colonies would offset the loss of trade and goodwill that would result. Thus, even a successful war would have been a net loss. But they could not stomach the humiliation of having their prestige and authority flouted by the colonial rascals. The need to reassert their power and status led the British into a war that cost them dearly.[16]

Similar patterns apply at the individual level. If someone causes you to lose face, you probably will seek revenge of some sort. Here, too, studies have shown that people will go to great lengths and accept tangible losses to get even.[17] The determining factor often seems to be how much people feel they are losing face. If someone has caused you trouble or cost you money, you may be angry and may try to get even, but you probably will not want to lose even more of your resources in the quest for revenge. But if the person has also humiliated you in front of others, then you will be much more willing to accept losses and sacrifices for the sake of revenge. Thus, unpleasant emotional states—anger and humiliation—can cause you to seek retaliation even at a substantial cost to yourself if you have been made to look bad.

In the studies just mentioned, people were guided by short-term goals: ending the cause of embarrassment, countering the damage to their image, and getting even with the person who was responsible for their loss of face. In some cases, people made sacrifices to avoid looking bad in front of total strangers whom they never expected to see again, forfeiting money they could have used for some future pleasure or benefits. These results again fit the pattern of emphasizing short-term goals at the expense of long-term ones. Also, two obvious and important causal factors were a focus on the self in some unpleasant way and a highly aversive emotional state of anger or embarrassment. (What we are talking about here is revenge for recent insults by adults. In chapter 6 we discuss how people use self-defeat to obtain revenge for injuries incurred during childhood.)

The celebrated case of Jean Harris may be a good illustration of the self-destructive excesses that a person can be drawn to in seeking revenge for humiliation. Harris, the headmistress of a prestigious private school, had had a long-term relationship with Herman Tarnower, a doctor who had become famous for developing the so-called Scarsdale Diet. He began seeing another woman, one younger than Harris, and soon it appeared that he might break off his relationship with Harris to devote himself to the other woman. Embarrassed and humiliated over what people might think of her, Harris became increasingly distraught over the situation and finally concluded that she had no chance of winning Tarnower back, whereupon she shot him to death. She was convicted of premeditated murder and given the mandatory prison sentence of fifteen years to life.[18]

What did Harris accomplish? She gained revenge for her humiliation at Tarnower's hands—that is, for his dumping her in favor of another woman. But the eventual cost of her vengeance was tremendous. The man she loved was dead, and she went to prison. Her chances for finding love—with Tarnower or with any other man—were probably ended forever when she shot Tarnower, so both her career and her love life were destroyed by a moment's angry passion.

Thus, once again, self-defeating behavior results from a desire to avoid feeling bad about the self—in this case, the public self. It is painful to think that others are laughing at you or regarding you negatively. People will seek revenge, even at substantial material cost to themselves, in order to prevent that from happening. The cost makes this behavior self-defeating.

SHYNESS

Yet another example of self-defeating trade-offs is shyness. Nearly everyone has felt shy at some point, and about two out of every five people describe themselves as shy.[19] Shyness has been defined in various ways, but most definitions involve some combination of unpleasant emotion (such as social anxiety) and behavioral tendencies to avoid other people or to withdraw from social situations.[20]

Shy people are not committed loners or contented introverts. Most shy people definitely want to get along with others, to have friends and lovers, and to experience intimacy. But a fear of rejection often causes shy people to avoid taking a chance on trying to get to know others. They fear that they will make a bad impression and experience rejection, humiliation, ostracism, and anxiety.[21] They are painfully aware of how others perceive them, and they constantly fear that others are seeing them in a bad light. Shy people therefore focus on avoiding anything that might produce rejection or embarrassment. When they have to interact with others, they will nod and smile but not reveal anything very personal. If not required to interact, the shy person will often avoid others and withdraw from social situations.

Shy behavior is thus self-defeating, because shy people end up destroying their chances to become intimate with others.

The only way to get close to others is to approach them and to share oneself, but shy people do not approach others for fear of being rejected. They will not take the chance of being hurt. Consequently, shy people end up being relatively lonely, having relatively little sexual experience, and having few intimate, long-term, romantic relationships, as compared with nonshy people.[22] Shy people often are unhappy about their isolation, even if it is self-imposed.

A secondary problem is that shy people often fail to develop adequate social skills. A number of studies have shown that shy people are more awkward or unskilled in social situations. For example, they are slower to start conversations with others than are nonshy people. When they do converse, they say less than nonshy people, make less eye contact, reveal fewer emotions in their faces, and smile less. All of these things reduce the message of warmth and interest that encourages people to get to know and like each other.

As a result, shyness may become self-perpetuating. If you are a shy person, most likely you often feel an overriding fear of social rejection, so you tend to avoid other people. Unfortunately, this avoidance prevents you from learning how to make friends and become intimate with others. It becomes a vicious circle.

The trade-off in shy behavior, then, is often a matter of sacrificing long-term satisfactions of intimacy and friendship for the sake of short-term safety from anxiety and rejection. In the long run, the person may realize such behavior is a bad bargain and a mistake. Still, shyness fits the now-familiar pattern in self-destructive trade-offs: the benefits are immediate, while the costs become apparent only over the long run.

The tension between possible and definite outcomes is also apparent in shyness. By avoiding others, shy people achieve a fairly certain emotional security, at least in the short run.

Approaching others may make them nervous, scared, or anxious, but withdrawing guarantees safety from those feelings. On the other hand, a main reason to approach someone else, to go to a party, or to participate in social settings is the chance to meet others and make friends, a chance that may lead to a satisfying intimacy. This, obviously, is only a chance; most social encounters do not lead to intimate relationships, even if no one acts shyly at all. Once again, therefore, we have a self-defeating trade-off that involves taking a certain immediate benefit over a possible future cost.

The irony is that shy people avoid other people and social situations to feel safe and free from anxiety, but in the long run social avoidance generally means they will be alone, which will make it harder for them to feel safe and to avoid anxiety. It is a self-defeating way of protecting oneself. In the next chapter we focus on another misguided strategy for protecting oneself, namely, self-handicapping.

5
Self-handicapping

The devil made me do it.
—Comedian Flip Wilson's signature line for one of his characters

ASCRIBING human traits to something nonhuman is a favorite literary device for exposing human frailties. Aesop used this tool both to portray human nature and to propose lessons to live by. One of his more famous fables cautions against hubris, which leads to arrogance or boastfulness when people are blessed with talent, riches, or success.

The fable describes a footrace between two grossly mismatched competitors. The hare had long been teasing the tortoise for being slow. The tortoise, who initially ignored the hare's taunting, was ultimately goaded into challenging him to a race. The hare first thought that the challenge was a joke, but the tortoise insisted on racing, so off they went. Sensing little threat from his competitor, the hare decided to stop partway before finishing and fell asleep. Consequently, the indefatigable, tenacious tortoise was able to prevail. The moral: Slow and steady wins the race.

In addition to presenting an important lesson about the value of perseverance and the cost of arrogance, Aesop's fable could have had much to say about self-defeat had it focused on aspects of the tortoise's *challenge* and not just on the hare's arrogance. It would seem that the tortoise's response to the hare's taunting would, under normal circumstances, have been destined to yield humiliation and pain. Or would it? Actually, by initiating an ostensibly ludicrous—possibly self-defeating —challenge against the hare, the tortoise was in a no-lose situation. Hares are innately fast, whereas tortoises are naturally slow, so who would care if the tortoise lost? Every David who goes against a Goliath prays for an upset victory, but few expect to defeat their opponent, and most are not distraught after losing.

Considering the hare, on the other hand, raises some questions: What psychological benefits could he have gained from competing against someone of such obviously inferior ability as the tortoise? Can winning a mismatch boost your competence image? Hardly. Therefore, the hare had everything to lose and nothing to gain by getting into a contest of this sort. Conversely, the overmatched tortoise had everything to gain—in terms of psychological benefits—and nothing to lose by opposing a foe who needed to vanquish him merely to save face.

SELF-HANDICAPPING: MUDDYING THE ATTRIBUTIONAL WATERS

Paradoxically, the only way for the hare to gain self-esteem from racing an opponent such as the tortoise would have been to adopt a self-defeating strategy *other* than the one he followed in Aesop's fable. Specifically, to win at a psychological level, he would have had to hamper his chances of winning prior to the start of the race, not quit partway through the competition.

Had the hare run the race with his feet encumbered by shackles or with a heavy weight on his back, he clearly could not have run his best. Such self-imposed impediments to success, although self-destructive, often afford significant psychological advantages.

First, executing any test of competence under less-than-optimal conditions allows you to claim that external agents kept your innate abilities in check. By imposing a burden on your own efforts, therefore, you can set yourself up to blame any failure on that burden: without it, the outcome would have been very different. Moreover, should you prevail despite being impeded by external circumstances, your talents will be considered all the greater. This strategy of maintaining or enhancing self-esteem through a pattern of self-defeat is called self-handicapping.[1]

Self-handicapping was originally defined as "any action or choice of performance setting that enhances the opportunity to externalize (or excuse) failure and to internalize (reasonably accept credit for) success."[2] More specifically, it is any tactic that structures the context within which evaluations take place so as to obscure the meaning of test results or render useless any assessment of competence or ability, such as tests or other evaluations. The situations that a self-handicapper "gets into" (in reality, they are designed) look painful or problematic, but paradoxically, they sustain the self-handicapper's favorable image of competence or self-esteem.

Self-handicapping works in one of two ways: by self-handicappers finding or creating impediments that make successful performance less likely, or by withdrawing effort in order to invite probable failure.[3] Either way, the validity of subsequent evaluations is obscured, and self-handicappers' true abilities cannot be assessed because external factors (such as impediments or lack of effort) mask those abilities. By

creating this judgmental ambiguity, the self-handicapper succeeds in preserving the favorable competence image that ex-
isted before the evaluation.

The unique self-defeating style of self-handicappers has
been called a "Faustian bargain,"[4] after the literary figure
made famous especially by Goethe. Like Faust, many self-
handicappers make a bargain with the devil: in their case, seeking
to protect their competence images in the present and worry
about the consequences of their strategic self-defeating behavior later. Moreover, they often see the consequences of their
bargain as reversible: they can always stop the self-defeating
behavior sometime in the future, they believe, and their abilities
will once again shine through.

Routes to Self-handicapping

Alcohol is one of the most common self-handicapping agents
precisely because its effects are so transient.[5] More important,
its effects are well known and can be visible to others. Extremely intoxicated people may completely withdraw their efforts by, for example, loafing on a task or underpreparing
because of procrastination.[6] Self-handicappers can protect
their self-esteem by taking a time-out from performance re-
quirements while under the influence of alcohol. Through
inaction they invite probable failure by not doing what is
necessary to succeed—often the best way to avoid damage to
their self-image. Regardless of what handicapping agent is
used—be it alcohol or any other "devil" that can make you do
"it"—the goal is to find justifications other than the self for
personal shortcomings.

One patient, Jennifer, a thirty-two-year-old creative director
for a Boston-based advertising agency, was hospitalized with

a primary diagnosis of "atypical depression." Treatment revealed, however, that while she clearly suffered a depressed mood, fatigue, and an impaired capacity to think and concentrate, her primary disorder was self-handicapping. A key to understanding this woman's unique use of depressive symptomatology was that all signs of sadness and distractibility vanished around six o'clock every evening. In fact, her husband reported that before her admission to the hospital, "she was like a helpless baby from nine to five, and then when I'd return home from work for dinner, she'd be like a love-starved nymphomaniac all night long!" While a loss of libido (and appetite) is not necessary to form a diagnosis of depression, it is among the most obvious and prevalent symptoms of this disorder. Moreover, most diagnoses of depression rest on an observation that a patient's malaise is long-standing (two weeks' duration or more). This woman's marked increase in *joie de vivre* after the traditional close of business each day was, if nothing else, a psychiatric anomaly among the symptoms of the truly depressed.

Jennifer had become depressed eight months after winning an advertising industry award akin to an Oscar or Emmy. Although initially elated by the honor, she had gradually become anxious and withdrawn as kudos and job offers flooded her way. When her firm responded to the attempts to woo her away with increased cash compensation and other perks, Jennifer sank deeper into malaise. She began failing to attend meetings and forgetting appointments, and ultimately she voiced concern that she could no longer create ad campaigns "because my muse abandoned me." At times this distress brought her to tears, both publicly and privately, and she finally became so distressed that she refused to go to work altogether and stayed home in her pajamas.

Jennifer's insight into the manner in which she employed

depression as an agent in a self-handicapping strategy came during a psychotherapy session when she declared, "If I'm ever able to make it back to [her ad agency] I hope they realize that this mood sickness is the reason why I won't be winning awards for a while." When challenged to explain what she meant by that, she said, "You know the business world: it's 'what have you done for me *lately?*' that matters. Without my depression, I'd be a failure now; with it, I'm a success 'on hold' till it passes, and who knows how long that will be? I'd much rather be a success as a failure than fail at being a success."

USING SELF-HANDICAPPING TO "TRADE UP"

There was a time in American society when Jennifer and others who use symptoms to avoid the burden of excessive performance expectations could not have made a scot-free escape from censure. Suffering a psychiatric disorder such as depression was once highly stigmatized. Similarly, alcohol abusers were, until recently, thought to be sinful "boozers" and were actively reproached for their presumably evil ways. When this attitude toward alcoholism held sway, people went to great lengths to hide bouts of abusive drinking. Since modern medicine has determined that depression and alcoholism are diseases, a dramatic attitudinal shift has occurred.

People are now far more willing to acknowledge that they drink; some go so far as to advertise the fact in their autobiographies or discuss on daytime talk shows their visits to renowned alcoholism-treatment clinics. The shame of drinking has virtually vanished, but its known harmful effects are as real as ever, so self-handicappers are in an ideal position to claim alcohol abuse as a justification for undesirable outcomes rather than confront the possibility that they are deficient in some important way. In fact, the so-called medical model of alcoholism is so widely accepted that some people argue that they suffer from it as a means of *enhancing* their social status and self-image in order to avoid being stigmatized by more undesirable diagnoses.

For example, according to one study of spouse abuse, the majority of instances of wife beating are preceded by the husband's excessive use of alcohol. Moreover, the alcohol consumption appears to be strategic; the abusive husbands studied would "drink in order to provide an excuse for becoming violent."[7] Interestingly, both the abusive husbands and their abused wives employed the face-saving logic of self-handicapping theory to account for the husband's behavior: they attributed the beatings to the influence of Demon Alcohol, not to the character of the abuser.

Research into the attitudes of child molesters toward others convicted of the same crime demonstrates how self-handicapping allows a person to "trade up" from a negative character attribution to another, less degrading one. One researcher found that child molesters who claimed to have been drunk at the time of their offenses held negative attitudes toward those who said they were sober when committing their acts of abuse and those who denied committing any offense.[8] Quotes from convicted child molesters reflect not only their willingness but their *desire* to be regarded as alcohol abusers, demonstrating the self-serving way that this negative diagnosis can functionally replace the far more distasteful diagnosis of "child abuser": "If I were sober, it never would have happened." "I have an alcohol problem, not a sex problem." "Drinking is the reason. I could always get a woman. I can't figure it out. A man's mind doesn't function right when he's got liquor on it."[9]

In an investigation of college students who evaluated written vignettes about some drunk and some sober people, the students held the drunk ones less responsible and less blameworthy for causing an undesirable outcome than they did the sober ones.[10] Other symptoms can be used in self-handicapping strategies to achieve the same effect. According to another study, symptoms of depression mitigate responsibility for spouse abuse in the same way that alcohol intoxication does.[11] Research subjects who read reports of spouse abusers suffering depressive symptoms at the time of a beating judged them to less blameworthy for the consequences of their actions than batterers who were described as having no depressive problems.

In recent years Washington, D.C., has become a hotbed of self-handicapping. During the mid-1980s, the nation's capital, which purportedly has the highest per capita alcohol-consumption rate in the country,[12] was awash in elected officials who used a "devil made me do it" pattern of self-serving behavior to defend against a variety of charges for illegal activities. You might not think that officials elected on the basis of the public's confidence in them would advertise the fact that they suffered from a psychological disorder, but self-handicapping works that way. It is a unique self-defeating style that trades on the awareness that public perceptions of "badness" fluctuate just as tastes in clothes, cars, and cuisine do.

Former Representative Michael J. Meyers of Philadelphia fought expulsion from Congress for accepting bribes from an undercover FBI agent (who filmed the transaction); Meyers said that his reason had been impaired by two glasses of bourbon whisky. Shortly after Meyers's conviction, Representative John W. Jenrette of South Carolina was found guilty of the same bribery crime that had unseated Meyers. During his trial, Jenrette asserted that he was a verifiable alcoholic who had been treated at a Texas clinic for his disorder before accepting the bribe. On the basis of this history and the fact that he had been intoxicated during meetings to plan the bribe, Jenrette sought leniency from the court, claiming that there were mitigating circumstances. And while Jenrette was pleading his case, former Congressman Robert Bauman was defending himself against charges of sexual misconduct with a sixteen-year-old boy, claiming that he, too, had acted inappropriate while "under the influence." In contrast to Jenrette, Bauman succeeded in trading up. The federal prosecutor who brought charges against Bauman agreed to drop the matter on the condition that he seek treatment for alcoholism.

HITTING BOTTOM WHEN YOU REACH THE TOP

Self-handicapping is not motivated solely by a desire to create a censure-proof public image, nor by an awareness that negative status may be improved by attributing failure to agents or agencies outside the self. Clinical observations indicate that psychological distress that is never publicly aired usually serves as the impetus for self-handicapping strategies. In fact, the more severe cases of chronic self-handicapping are almost always caused by nagging, irrational doubts about competence or self-worth that people keep hidden from others.[13]

Paradoxically, ostensible good fortune is a primary cause of self-handicapping behavior. Recall that Deschapelles, the champion chessplayer described in chapter 1, designed his self-serving "coup" *after* he became champion of his region. And as outfielder Darryl Strawberry of the New York Mets observed when teammate Dwight Gooden responded to a stellar pitching season by abusing cocaine, "Success is great, but then everything hits the fan."[14]

This type of success-induced self-defeat occurs for many reasons. Certain kinds of success experiences render a person who "has it all" more vulnerable to the fear of "losing it all."[15] Specifically, successes thought to be a function of extraneous factors such as luck, "connections," beauty, or birthright—as opposed to personal attributes such as ability or intelligence—heighten the motivation for self-handicapping. The less people believe that they can exert direct control over the factors that produce a successful outcome, the more likely they are to handicap themselves when required to sustain their successful status or replicate successful performances.

Noncontigent Success

Psychologists call the type of success experience that is likely to promote self-handicapping a "noncontingent" success, because people who experience it cannot establish a linkage (contingency) between their instrumental, goal-directed behaviors and the rewarding outcome.[16] Instead of *achieving* a desired result, people who experience noncontingent success feel that they are *receiving* success—like "pennies from heaven"—for attributes or factors beyond their control. When someone lands a job, receives a promotion, or wins a contest solely because of an external attribute such as inherited physical beauty, the result is often anxiety, doubt, and questions about self-worth.

When researchers first investigated the role played by noncontingent success in precipitating self-handicapping behavior, they designed an experimental paradigm to mimic "pennies from heaven."[17] Specifically, some subjects in the original studies of self-handicapping received success feedback that was completely noncontingent, while the other subjects received the same feedback but did so the old fashioned way; they *earned* it.

Volunteers reported for an alleged test of the effects of two drugs on intellectual functioning. One drug supposedly enhanced intellectual performance, whereas the other drug supposedly impaired intellectual functioning much as alcohol would. The experimenter told subjects that in order to determine whether either of the two (actually bogus) drugs affected intellectual performance, it would be necessary to follow what is known as a test/retest protocol: each subject's intellectual competence would first be assessed free from extraneous influences to establish a baseline and then again under the influence of one of the drugs, which the subject would choose.

The subjects were then given a battery of problems that resembled those typically found on IQ tests or the Scholastic Aptitude Test and were told that they would be receiving twenty problems to solve before taking a drug and twenty from the same battery after the drug entered their systems and had time to "take effect." In reality, however, only half the subjects took an authentic test. To create conditions of noncontingent success, the remaining subjects received a test battery containing problems that appeared to be authentic but were, in fact, virtually all unsolvable. Try as they might, these subjects were forced to guess on 80 percent of the questions they received.

Once the "initial" test battery was administered, all the subjects were told—regardless of the questions they had received—"You did extraordinarily well on the first half of the test. Actually, yours is the highest score I've seen to date—sixteen out of twenty correct. Congratulations! Now, which drug would you like to receive prior to the retest of your intellectual ability?"

By telling all subjects that they had performed exceptionally

well on the initial test battery, the experimenter created conditions of both contingent success (for those subjects who received solvable questions) and noncontingent success (for
those whose questions were unsolvable). As predicted, approximately 67 percent of the male subjects in the noncontingent success condition handicapped themselves by choosing
the performance-inhibiting drug before a retest of their abilities. Less than 20 percent of the males receiving contingent
success feedback chose this option. For reasons still not understood (since female self-handicappers are well known to
mental health professionals and the public at large), female
subjects did not behave similarly.

In one study of self-handicapping behavior in a psychiatric
hospital setting, nearly 20 percent of the patients being treated
for alcoholism were found to have a background that conformed to the self-handicapping dynamic.[18] These patients—
roughly half, women—reported a history of noncontingent
success (for example, inherited wealth but no career success;
beauty or family connections resulting in positions of status
with no comparable *achieved* successes) before their alcohol
abuse. In addition, most of these alcohol abusers were aware
that their drinking problems had begun immediately before an
event that threatened either to strip them of their status or to
"expose" their lack of merit or competence.

Apparently, the problem with succeeding because of who
you are, as opposed to what you have accomplished, is that you
are uncertain of your ability to replicate the conditions that
accounted for your past success if you are called on to succeed
again. If, for example, you are made a corporate officer because the corporation's board of directors knows your uncle,
who happens to be a state senator, a different board installed
following a corporate takeover may be less favorably disposed
to you and, through no fault of yours, may replace you. By

experiencing noncontingent success, you would have to cope with this threat to your competence image and be ever vigilant to further threats posed by repeated assessments of your ability. In contrast, if you became a corporate officer after salvaging the fortunes of two losing business ventures, you would suffer far fewer concerns about being replaced if the board of directors changed.

Beauty Contests and Political Victories

Comparable concerns arise when you win a contest because of who or what you are rather than because of what you are capable of doing. Actress Candice Bergen has fought a lifelong battle against the anxiety and expectations imposed on her by being strikingly beautiful and winning roles partly because of this attribute. As she has observed, "People who don't have it think beauty is a blessing. Actually, it's a kind of sentence, a confinement. It sets you apart. People see you as an object, not as a person, and they project a set of expectations onto that object."[19] Psychoanalysts agree. Several case studies of objectively beautiful women involved in psychotherapy found that in addition to depression and involvement in various forms of self-defeating behavior, the one experience common to this group was the sense that they were deprived of their humanity by the expectations generated by their looks.[20]

The metaphor of winning a beauty contest on looks or charisma alone captures the essence of many political contests and can help explain why Washington seems to be home to so many self-handicappers. In the political arena, success is often gained noncontingently through the political "winds of fortune." Winning a political race has little in common with a legitimate footrace; only racers who start with equal opportunities to win experience contingent success. In politics there is one inescapable truth: Getting to the top is more a function of *who* you are than *what* you have done. Although successful politicians often possess internal strengths such as perseverance, intelligence, and altruism that can account for their long terms in office, most political successes—as recent presidential campaigns have demonstrated—are more appropriately attributed to image consultants, media strategists, speechwriters, and campaign directors—the people who shape the candidate's *outside* rather than exposing his or her professional, psychological *inside*.

Politicians are also prone to engaging in self-handicapping strategies because they constantly face impending evaluations (elections) that threaten to strip them of previously acquired esteem. Any elected official who remains in office very long or strives for higher office faces the risk of being unseated if the political climate shifts. What better way to protect their competence image and ensure a legacy of prestige than to quit while they are ahead or, better yet, create the no-lose image protection afforded by self-handicapping?

Recall that when former Senator Gary Hart was caught cavorting with Donna Rice, he was quick to use the ambiguity caused by his ostensibly self-destructive action to his advantage: his womanizing became an ideal self-handicapping agent. When driven from the 1988 race for the presidency, Hart argued that he was leaving because journalists were making his character, not his platform, the focus of their coverage. He could claim that the press, not his own actions, cost him the Democratic nomination and, moreover, that had his ideas been heard over the din, he would have been a very good president.

Since Hart could blame an external handicap (Rice-induced harassment) for his failure to reach the Oval Office, his self-defeating behavior left him positioned for a future move: Phoenix-like, he may emerge from the ashes of his political career and claim that his "disease" is behind him and that he is prepared to be a politician once again. A resurrection of this sort would be much more difficult if Hart had left office after losing an election in which the voters found his abilities lacking, for it is much harder to compensate for an internal deficiency than to demonstrate victory over an external problem.

WHEN TOO MUCH OF A GOOD THING CAN BE BAD

A second type of success experience known to precipitate self-handicapping strategies has little to do with why a person was rewarded but instead concerns the *nature* of the rewarding outcomes. It has been called "excessive" noncontingent success and can best be described as an "avalanche of riches."[21] The problem with this ostensibly favorable outcome is that it is known to be as psychologically disruptive as an avalanche on a ski slope. Excessive noncontingent successes ultimately motivate patterns of self-serving self-defeat because they far exceed the level of rewards normally associated with a particular endeavor. People who receive windfalls often experience psychological stress and anxiety over the responsibility of living up to the expectations generated by these rewards. Not only must they produce at a level that will justify what has been earned but—given the nature of most success-induced expectations (for example, "What have you done for me lately?")—they face the threat of having to improve on past performances.

Even the intensity of the limelight garnered by an excessive noncontingent success can prove disquieting because of the psychological changes it can cause. Chief among these is the disruptive psychological experience called objective self-awareness.[22] As we saw in chapter 3, focusing on the self is often uncomfortable—so much so that it can generate a drive to escape circumstances that heighten self-awareness, because it is likely to expose our faults or deficiencies. Moreover, since recipients of excessive noncontingent success know that they do not measure up to the implications of the rewards they have received, that pressure, added to objective self-awareness, may hasten their drive to an ill-conceived, maladaptive form of escape like alcohol.

It is here that self-destructive patterns of substance abuse can be doubly self-serving. On the one hand, self-handicapping is a virtually fool-proof way for people to take themselves off the hot seat generated by heightened performance expectations, since it affects performance capabilities. On the other hand, alcohol derives much of its reinforcing potential from the fact that it reduces states of heightened self-awareness.[23] When superstars like Judy Garland, Truman Capote, and Tennessee Williams fall from glorious heights to self-induced destruction, it is often the combined influence of two forms of self-serving self-defeating behavior—the drive to protect self-esteem through self-handicapping and the drive to lower objective self-awareness—that initiates their descent. People who find themselves stressed by the pressures of reaching the pinnacle of success are not *aiming* for the bottom; they are actually seeking quick relief from psychological pain when they drink. The problem is they do not calculate the long-term consequences of their actions when bargaining with this devil.

THE PAIN OF PASSIVITY

A final problem with the rewards of success that deserves special attention is attaining goals too easily. People who achieve contingent successes and are rewarded appropriately may still experience distress if the task lacked adequate *challenge*.[24] Shooting fish in a barrel will neither improve people's sense of self-esteem nor generate the feeling that they can control significant aspects of their world—what psychologists call self-efficacy.[25] More important, effortless successes cannot make the world feel like a safe or joyful place. The poet Robert Browning said, "Ah, but a man's reach should exceed his grasp, / Or what's a heaven for?" Yet many who assume that heaven awaits them when they achieve success find that the aftermath is sheer boredom if they attained their goal effortlessly.[26]

Seeking out demanding competition is the ideal way to ensure that your reach will exceed your grasp and that success will provide feelings of self-efficacy. Many people, however, try to add thrills to effortless success through less adaptive, often self-destructive means. Ivan Boesky, Martin Siegel, and Michael Milken are easily recognizable names because, despite receiving compensation packages in excess of $1 million per year, their insider-trading ring broke several laws—and ended their careers—for sums as paltry (to them) as $700,000. In their field—investment banking—seven-figure salaries were neither unique nor particularly prestigious. In the booming 1980s it took far more than $1 million to mark someone as a "breed apart." While greed is the most widely proffered explanation for what these men did, their self-destructive behavior may best be understood as an attempt to dare the proverbial devil and beat him.

Without overanalyzing the careers of those involved in the

insider-trading scandal, we can say that their fortunes were clearly made with relative ease once they reached senior positions on Wall Street. As top-level specialists who funded corporate refinancing, buyouts, and mergers, they had deals brought to them. After being handed business, they had little trouble—or challenge—putting together the financing, and their countless assistants with M.B.A.s or comparable degrees did much of the work for them. If all it took to engineer a $1-million consulting fee were a warm smile and a well-stocked Rolodex, what authentic gain in self-esteem could that provide? Boesky and others like him knew that the nuts and bolts of their operation were handled by others and, as a consequence, felt little enhancement of their self-worth when a deal was done. But if the inside traders had succeeded in keeping their scam undetected, they would have reveled in the knowledge that they had beat the system and the odds in favor of getting caught; *that* would have truly been a coup.

We stress again that self-handicappers such as these are not engaging in patterns of self-defeat intended to engineer their demise. Self-serving patterns of self-defeat are initiated despite *foreseeable* harm because they can relieve immediate distress, but their harm is not intended. Instead, it seems as though self-handicappers have a pathological investment in their sense of self-worth. They will go to great lengths to preserve it and to relieve transient demands that threaten it. More specifically, self-handicappers are so exquisitely vulnerable to the slights and bruises that can accompany failure that avoiding these negative outcomes ultimately becomes more important to them than achieving success.

Therein lies the dilemma of all self-handicappers: Although their ultimate goal is to maintain or enhance their competence *image,* the pattern of self-serving self-defeat that they employ involves undermining skilled behavior or impeding the execution of complex tasks that, if mastered, reflect their underlying abilities.[27] Self-handicappers do not set out primarily to ensure failure; they are willing to accept probable failure if it can be explained away or can position them to enhance their self-esteem by prevailing against the odds.

FAILING BY NOT TRYING

Self-handicappers include not only people who have reached the pinnacle of their professions but also many whose careers have become derailed en route to the top. Their self-serving patterns of self-defeat are commonly observed in clinical practices that specialize in treating underachievers. One representative example of this style, Doug, a fifty-four-year-old *magna cum laude* graduate of a top university, entered psychotherapy to learn how to cope better with work supervisors who were, from his perspective, jealous of his intellectual brilliance. Despite an obvious capacity to perform all job tasks required of him in his midlevel accounting positions, Doug had recently been fired for the eighth time in his career. Yet rather than examining his role in precipitating his firings, Doug sought to place the blame for his plight squarely on the shoulders of those who had wielded the axe. Specifically, he maintained that supervisors let him go because they feared that he would take their jobs.

Soon after his evaluative psychotherapy session, it became obvious that while this man indeed possessed rare intellectual gifts, his failed career had nothing to do with intimidating those above him. It turned out that he was chronically absent from the office and that when he was there, he regularly failed to complete assignments on time. Doug attributed both his absenteeism and his procrastination to a back ailment that interfered with his sleep, often prevented him from driving his car to his place of work (which in every case was inaccessible by public transportation), and made it difficult for him to sit still at his desk for lengthy periods. Not surprisingly, psychotherapy with Doug was initiated by focusing on why he had never sought surgical treatment or physical therapy for the slipped disc he had suffered from for thirty years.

The simple answer was that by allowing his back ailment to flourish without medical attention, Doug exploited a handicap that enabled him to protect the competence image he had achieved in college from potentially negative feedback that he might receive in the workplace. Doug traded physical pain, plus the costs and chagrin of chronic unemployment and job seeking, for the psychological security of never having his sense of competence and self-worth challenged. To use a baseball analogy, because he was prevented regularly from showing up at the ballpark capable of batting to the best of his ability, he could convince himself that he never really struck out.

Excessively Good Samaritans

Although the type of self-handicapping style typified by Doug usually exploits physical agents or conditions that directly affect a person's capacity to perform competently, other people can also serve as handicaps. In fact, many self-serving self-defeatists actively exploit the personality flaws of those close to them in order to mask or justify their own shortcomings and, in so doing, achieve a variety of self-protective ends. A number of self-serving patterns of self-defeat are accomplished with some form of altruism: excessive caring for another person is used to engineer a self-inflicted demise. Such

Good Samaritans in effect play a role better described as that of Excessively Good Samaritans. They use a chronic, all-consuming devotion to another person as a handicap that prevents them from doing challenging activities in which their competency would be evaluated.

Psychiatrist Eric Berne maintains that these people exploit a strategic self-presentational ploy that involves proclaiming: "If it weren't for you . . . (I'd be a success, wealthy, and so on)."[28] In so doing, self-serving self-defeatists lay the blame for their failure on the actions or influence of others—most typically, loved ones—whom they begrudgingly but faithfully serve and stay associated with. By assuming the onus of a parent or spouse, Excessively Good Samaritans can ensure that they will be impeded from doing things that might lead to failure.

Excessively Good Samaritans are notable for their failure to extricate themselves from responsibilities to others—such as an ailing parent or a chemically dependent spouse—even when they have the resources to do so (for example, by sharing responsibilities with a sibling or hiring a private-duty nurse). By arranging to incur the pain of being hampered by responsibility to another person, these self-saboteurs avoid having their privately held notions of competence challenged and thereby maintain an illusion of future success.

Certain Excessively Good Samaritans stay overly connected to possessive, demanding parents because the performance arena they fear striking out in is marriage. Many "devoted" children stay tied to their parents in what can only be called a self-serving self-protective strategy that relieves anxiety about finding a potential mate. These people lament the need to support their aging parents, but they experience relief in believing they would have had wonderful relationships and in never confronting the morbid fear of failure in those.

DO SELF-HANDICAPPERS FEAR
SUCCESS?

A popular explanation for self-handicappers' behavior is that this type of self-defeating dynamic is motivated by a desire to avoid the guilt-induced, imaginary, negative consequences that would come from reaching a goal: in short, a fear of success.[29] Freud observed that many of his patients were, in his words, "wrecked by success." The most widely cited of these case studies describe a pattern of psychological decompensation the moment a patient reaches a goal that actualizes a long-held dream. One representative case from Freud's practice included a girl who "began to go to pieces" and later fell "into incurable mental illness" after a man with whom she was living asked her to marry him. Another involved a highly competent university professor who "cherished the wish" to succeed the man who had initiated and shaped his academic career. When he was chosen to fill the chair vacated by his mentor's retirement, the professor began to deprecate his own abilities and fell into a state of severe depression that prevented him from working.[30]

Freud explained these and related phenomena entirely in terms of unresolved Oedipal guilt. As we discussed in chapter 1, Freud assumed that success of any stripe—be it marrying or reaching the pinnacle of a profession—represents or recalls an Oedipal victory in which the child is presumed to triumph over the same-sex parent, enabling the child to assume a prized (sexual or romantic) position with the parent of the opposite sex. While some gains obviously come from victories of this sort, they are clearly outweighed by the debilitating fear that the more powerful parent of the same sex will seek retribution.

Freudian theory also maintains that unless a person successfully resolves Oedipal guilt by relinquishing a desire for the opposite-sex parent, residual guilt over fantasized or actual vanquishing of the same-sex parent will cause all manifestations of success to assume life-threatening proportions. Thus, when people who suffer this form of guilt sabotage success, it is assumed that their goal is to preempt feared retaliation symbolically. They preserve a known level of safety in exchange for the potential rewards that might come from successes.

Other Psychoanalytic Perspectives

While we agree that people will engage in self-defeating behavior to trade success for safety, we think the concept of guilt is overused as a reason for this. One guilt-free explanation of this type of self-defeating strategy was advanced in the 1950s by the eminent psychiatrist H. S. Sullivan.[31]

From Sullivan's so-called interpersonal perspective on psychiatry, all forms of self-defeating behavior emerge in response to a problematic relationship between child and mother known as a "separation-individuation" conflict. Simply stated, Sullivan's theory holds that a critical determinant of a child's self-conception comes from the way his mother responds to his earliest strivings for, or manifestations of, independence. If a mother responds to her child's pursuit of autonomy with anger or hostility—as though she were being rejected or rebuffed—or if she shows anxiety over the child's attempts to achieve self-mastery, her child will view worldly success very ambivalently. Despite the sense of power, freedom, and joy that independence can afford a young child, if it causes his mother to experience emotional distress, it ultimately acquires the potential to exact severe emotional penalties for the child in terms of lost security, abandonment, or rejection by a loved and needed parent.

Sullivan recognized that a readily available solution to this separation-individuation conflict can be found in self-defeat. By sabotaging the actions that will secure his independence and consequently cost him love, an anxious child can reestablish a secure relationship with his mother by failing to succeed. In essence, this model is identical to our self-serving pattern of self-defeat except for its claim that all self-defeat is intended to reestablish ties with a neurotic mother and its linkage to a flawed parent-child interaction initiated in earliest childhood.

Obvious Reinforcers of Self-handicapping

Since many of the self-handicappers we see do not initiate self-defeating styles until adulthood—many doing so only after long strings of successes—we feel that Sullivan's perspective, while a significant improvement over Freud's, still fails as an all-encompassing explanation for self-serving self-defeat. Success brings with it enough real-world stressors that we see no need to look for deeply repressed neurotic conflicts in accounting for the initiation of all self-handicapping behavior. Obviously, any given self-handicapper—for example, a grade school student with an IQ of 155 who fails all his tests the week after he is taunted by classmates for being a teacher's pet—may wish to establish a closer tie with his mother or feel guilt for displacing his father within an Oedipal triangle. But we believe that the *obvious* reinforcer—relief from social ostracism—that self-imposed failure can afford this underachiever is the more specific and useful explanation for this style of self-destructive behavior and for comparable patterns in which self-esteem can be protected by inflicting harm to other aspects of the self.

THE PSYCHOLOGY BEHIND THE DESCHAPELLES COUP

As we saw at the beginning of this chapter, one important added benefit gained by self-saboteurs who employ self-handicapping strategies is the possibility of not failing when under the influence of a performance-inhibiting agent. This is one way they enhance their competence image. Since their goal is to create uncertainty about their actual competence, they undertake challenging activities with one hand figuratively tied behind their back. If they fail to perform as expected, observers will attribute their incompetence to the handicapping agent and never know how well they could have performed using two hands. But should they succeed *despite* the inhibiting actions of a handicapping agent, attributions of their inherent, underlying competence will soar.[32] This is what Deschapelles had in mind by sacrificing "pawn and move" to opponents when he was unsure of beating them. If he prevailed against self-imposed impediments to success, his ability would be rated all the higher.

Varying Motives

Because self-handicapping offers a double benefit—both discrediting failure and amplifying success—some researchers have asked which motive is the true or predominant one. The answer appears to depend on the personality of the self-handicapper. According to one recent series of experimental studies, people with low self-esteem engage in self-handicapping to protect themselves against failure; people with high self-esteem engage in the same actions to enhance their credit for success.[33] This difference probably is related to the way these two kinds of people approach life in general. People with high self-esteem tend not to worry about failure as much as others, because they do not expect to fail. But people with low self-esteem often feel that they can and do fail at things, and so the need for self-protection becomes central.

In the studies university students went to a laboratory for a project allegedly concerned with developing a new intelligence test. Half of these students were told that the (actually nonexistent) new test they would take was being designed as a screening device to identify potential geniuses. They were told that the test discriminated only between the truly gifted and everyone else. There was thus no way to "fail" at the test; they could either succeed immensely or receive an inconclusive result. In other words, the test could not prove them to be stupid, but it could prove they were geniuses—a no-lose situation. Under these conditions, people with high self-esteem were far more likely to engage in self-handicapping than other people. Their self-handicapping took the form of withholding effort, failing to practice, and (in one study) choosing to listen to a style of music that they had been told would impair their performance. People with high self-esteem gave themselves these obstacles to increase the credit they would receive if they succeeded.

The other half of the students in the experiments were told that the new test was designed to identify intellectually inferior people. These people thus faced a radically different situation: for them, failure—that is, being identified as intellectually inferior—was a real possibility, but there was no way to succeed. The experimenter even said that if someone were a little below average, the test results would still be inconclusive, because the test was reliable only in identifying seriously inferior cases. In this situation, people with low self-esteem used self-handicapping strategies. They were apparently worried about failing and were therefore careful to give themselves an excuse (such as disruptive music or inadequate practice) in case they should fail. Why did people with high self-esteem not show self-handicapping in that situation? Probably because they did not think they would fail and so felt no need to have an excuse ready.

These findings refute the notion that self-saboteurs, particularly self-handicappers, are inherently losers. As we have said in earlier chapters, self-defeating behaviors are often initiated by people who have accomplished a great deal. Moreover, self-sabotaging behaviors often initially yield rewarding effects that only later lead to pain and suffering. The problem encountered by self-serving self-defeatists is that after engaging in actions that are adaptive in the short term, they fail to modify their behavior patterns once circumstances (most often, threats to self-esteem) change.

Distress and Eustress

When psychologists examine how people secure self-esteem enhancement or joy from success, they often focus on the degree of challenge or threat contained in a performance. Researchers have shown that when the demand to perform threatens our sense of safety or psychological integrity, we experience the form of stress familiar to most people, the type associated with disease causation and properly called distress. There is, however, a beneficial form of stress that can enhance both physical and psychological health. When people are challenged to perform at peak potential—that is, when they test their abilities by pitting themselves against performance standards or worthy opponents—successful outcomes can lead to feelings of well-being, called eustress.[34]

There is often a fine line between stimuli that generate

feelings of eustress and those that cause distress, since excessive challenges often become threatening. Thus, a novice skier may progress from the "bunny hill" to a beginner's course to an intermediate slope and upward, all the while gaining self-esteem and feelings of eustress from mastering the ever-increasing challenges of steeper and steeper hills. Yet if that same skier continues to the expert run, the performance demand may become threatening and precipitate feelings of distress.

Self-handicappers do not need to don ski boots and bear the cold in order to enhance the challenges in their lives and thus obtain feelings of eustress. They can adopt a range of symptoms or suffer various psychological disorders guaranteed to make it more challenging for them to do well. The most common of these disorders is procrastination, a form of trade-off already discussed in chapter 4. Underpreparing for an evaluation can add challenge to the process of striving for success. Most of us can recall being in a classroom on the day of an examination when a grade-hungry student has announced—in an aside to no one in particular yet loud enough for all to hear—that she would "bomb" the test because she first started studying for it only that morning. When the test came back, she could be expected to claim that if she had not procrastinated, her grade of 90 would surely have been 100. Actually, her contention may have been more accurate than not despite its obnoxious qualities, for the high level of self-esteem that would lead her to self-handicap to enhance success would likely have been based on earlier academic successes.

Managing Expectations

The renowned philosopher and psychologist William James proposed a formula for determining a person's level of self-esteem: divide successes by pretensions.[35] (When James used the term *pretensions* it did not connote affectations, haughty displays, or presumptuous assertions, as it does today. Instead, it was used essentially as a synonym for *expectations*.) To enhance self-esteem, all you need to do is increase success or lower pretensions. Since increasing success on meaningful tasks is no simple matter, the way to regulate self-esteem is obviously to address pretensions.

Self-handicappers "regulate pretension" when they report for evaluations under the influence of performance-inhibiting agents or self-imposed obstacles to success. By heightening the likelihood that they will suffer defeat, they lower their pretentions (that is, their expectations for success). Once they do that, all they need to do to experience an enhanced competence image is to perform as they would have prior to adopting the handicap. Once again we see how a person can augment self-esteem by engaging in a self-serving self-defeating behavior.

A variant of this technique occurs quite commonly in settings such as professional sports or the performing arts, in which people face ongoing scrutiny or assessment. It involves using a characterological or dispositional handicap—typically, some form of performance anxiety—to preserve or protect one's reputation.[36] Many performers who develop conditions that force them to quit the fast track prematurely discover that they have augmented the image of their competence that is preserved for history.

The legend of Greta Garbo may be a case in point. In 1941, at age thirty-six, she left Hollywood and moviemaking after the failure of *Two-Faced Woman*. According to many reports, she never planned a permanent retirement, but she never actively opposed one either. In fact, projects that fell through because of factors such as financing could have been completed if Garbo had determined that circumstances were right. As one insightful movie critic noted, "The moody, private Garbo, who always hated the fuss of fame, found it easier to wander aimlessly through the rest of her life than test herself against her own increasingly burdensome legend."[37]

Some researchers have shown that shyness can be a highly effective self-handicapping agent.[38] Seen from our vantage point, Garbo used her shyness as a self-serving self-defeating strategy designed to shield her from a public that would examine and, worse yet, evaluate her. In essence, her withdrawal from public scrutiny lowered the objective self-awareness that her inordinate fame induced. Yet through this ultimately self-defeating process, Garbo augmented her public image from that of a movie star to that of a film legend or, some say, screen goddess. The reputation that she established in her twenty-four successful movies was left to grow essentially unchallenged by her one flop. To use another baseball analogy, hers was a strategy of not going to the ballpark—and not going to bat—which served to avoid the possibility of striking out.

The psychology underlying Garbo's evaluation avoidance is identical to that of many people who suffer debilitating levels of test anxiety. These people defeat their chances to achieve ongoing success by claiming that their disease prevents them from reporting for valid assessments of their true potential.[39] This type of disorder, offered in lieu of transient handicaps such as the influence of alcohol, lack of adequate preparation, or lack of sleep, is convenient for many self-handicappers who anticipate encountering ongoing evaluations.

Self-handicappers occupy a unique status in the family of self-saboteurs because of their ability to create no-lose esteem-protective strategies that, for the most part, exact a relatively mild physical toll. By structuring evaluative interactions to make it appear that they have a hand tied behind their back at all times, they minimize the negative implications of failure and maximize the positive implications that result from success. Although self-handicapping can cause permanent damage—from substance abuse, white-collar crime, or chronic patterns of psychiatric disorders such as anxiety or depression—the self-defeatist who adopts such behavior is motivated by the belief that the trade-off will yield an enhanced sense of self-esteem or social esteem. In the next chapter we examine a far more debilitating pattern of self-defeat that, rather than addressing competence or self-image concerns, apparently arises from an unresolved sense of having been wronged.

6
Pyrrhic Revenge

Another such victory over the Romans, and we are undone.
—Pyrrhus, king of Epirus, following his defeat of a Roman army

WHEN King Pyrrhus of Greece made his wry remark in 280 B.C., he could hardly have guessed that he would be associated to this very day with costly victories. Actually, the concept of a Pyrrhic victory is more closely associated with winning at a *ruinous* cost, so that no one seems to have won the battle. The divorcing husband and wife played by Michael Douglas and Kathleen Turner in the movie *War of the Roses* exemplify this dynamic. Rather than divide their property and civilly go their separate ways, each endures the aggressive contempt and physical abuse of the other in hopes of retaining possession of their home and precious belongings. When it is all over, the two combatants lie exhausted among the ruins of what was once a million-dollar residence, their material wealth and peace of mind a shambles.

As mentioned in chapter 1, the maliciously intentioned style of self-defeat that draws its name from Pyrrhus's military conquest—Pyrrhic revenge—results in ruinous outcomes for those who initiate it, yet there are crucial distinctions between battles waged by armies and those waged by self-saboteurs.

First, we call these tactics Pyrrhic *revenge,* rather than Pyrrhic *victory,* because the underlying motive seems to be intentional payback rather than current conquest. Although Pyrrhic-revenge strategies may be directed at those responsible (in the mind of the self-saboteur) for the psychological distress that prompts them, self-saboteurs often use this self-defeating style in a unconscious attempt to avenge abuse inflicted on them by a parent now deceased or absent.[1] Despite appearances to the contrary, the pain and suffering regularly meted out to spouses or other parent substitutes (such as lovers or bosses) is actually a self-saboteur's maladaptive attempt to right various wrongs suffered during childhood.

Second, in contrast to most Pyrrhic victories that leave combatants wondering, What did I gain from all this? Pyrrhic revenge appears to provide immediate, short-term gratification. Pyrrhic revenge is accomplished in a variety of ways that share one common, defining component: the capacity to harm another while harming the self. By initiating a battle, creating a mutually harmful circumstance, or provoking costly retaliatory gestures, Pyrrhic-revenge strategies provide psychological reinforcement or relief that in some way compensates significantly for the overt harm to the self.

One patient who exhibited a Pyrrhic-revenge self-defeating style deserves special attention. Jerry entered therapy at age twenty-six for help with a self-diagnosed "gambling addiction." Before that he had been hospitalized at four different addiction-treatment facilities for a total of nearly one year of inpatient therapy for this disorder. The hospitalizations had failed miserably; Jerry calculated that he had lost over $1 million gambling on anything from horse races to elections. In fact, inpatient therapy had been so ineffectual that even during his hospitalizations he often found a way to call bets in to bookmakers.

Jerry was the fifth and last child born to a very wealthy New

England industrialist father, who headed a manufacturing conglomerate founded by Jerry's grandfather, and a mother who, according to Jerry, was "your basic housewife." All of Jerry's siblings shared in the family business: his brother ran an out-of-state division of the business, and his sisters' husbands all held executive-level positions in the company. Although emotionally distant from one another (for example, they would gather as a group only on Christmas Eve), Jerry and his siblings never competed for parts of the family business—there was much more than enough to go around, and Jerry's father spread it generously. In fact, Jerry's family were such active philanthropists that a church recreation facility had been named in their honor.

Jerry had graduated from college with a degree in economics and, because he liked finance, was being groomed to become the chief financial officer of the corporation—someone who would report directly to his father, the president and chief executive officer. Essentially, he had everything a young person could hope for: a guaranteed career, inherited wealth, friends, and physical health. Yet for some mysterious—and incredibly treatment-resistant—reason he was repeatedly derailed by gambling.

After his first hospitalization Jerry was promised that he could reassume his position in the family business "if he cleaned up his act," but his status eroded as he repeatedly found himself forced to ask his father tearfully for money to cover his gambling losses. These encounters almost always resulted in three specific responses by Jerry's father. First, he would scream and verbally abuse Jerry for his "damned ignorance" (in placing bets and hoping to win); then he would cry and give Jerry the six-figure "advances" needed to cover the debts; finally, he would curse the previous psychiatric caregivers who had failed his son and would search for yet another "competent" psychotherapist to care for his boy.

During his evaluative interview Jerry noted that his father was "intensely concerned" that Jerry was "unable to handle the company's books [because of] this betting problem." He then went on to swear, repeatedly, that he would "lick, once and for all" his compulsive gambling, in order to reassume his place in the corporate hierarchy. Yet the most significant disclosure that occurred during that session was not an insight into the urges or impulses that prompted him to place ill-advised, typically losing bets. The statement that guided his psychotherapy proved to be the tearful confession: "What kills me—tears my guts out—about this disease is what it's doing to my family. When my dad has to deal with those low-life scum bookies—paying them off with the profits from the business that my grandfather built with his own two hands—the pain is so great that I could die. Actually, it's not my pain that hurts—I'll pay my debt; I'll sell my [company] stock—it's seeing the tortured look on my Dad's face and seeing him cry that gets me. I know I'm stabbing him in the gut with a knife when I gamble."

How right he was. In fact, Jerry's disorder became easy to diagnose (yet remained difficult to treat) when the unique aspects of his gambling episodes were identified. Although Jerry believed that he had an addiction to gambling, he failed to meet the criteria established by the American Psychiatric Association for a "pathological gambling" disorder.[2] Pathological gamblers are preoccupied with gambling, are restless or irritable if they cannot gamble, and chronically increase the size or frequency of wagers in order to achieve a state of excitement from gambling. Jerry's gambling was quite different: he gambled only very intermittently; and when he placed bets and won, he never felt "high." If he went on a "gambling jag," as he called it, he would make only one type of wager (almost always $10,000 per event) and would repeat this pattern virtually nonstop until he found himself in so much debt that he was forced to contact his father for help. The most distinctive feature of Jerry's gambling career, however, was the fact that *every* jag was precipitated by feelings of rage toward his father. Jerry was suffering from a character disturbance best described as maliciously intentioned self-defeat.

Despite being a pillar of the community and an indisputable financial success, Jerry's father was cold, rebuking, and hostile to his son. He had been nearly fifty years old when Jerry was born, and according to one of Jerry's sisters, "Dad never had time for the 'little dynamo' scampering hither and yon." More important, he was cruel to Jerry, who, as the youngest of five children, seemed perennially to get little of his father's time and attention. Jerry reported that his dad never attended a single one of his choir recitals or art exhibitions from elementary school through college, and despite constant pleas, Jerry's father would never spend "nonbusiness" time with him. In fact, when Jerry attempted to interact with his dad outside the corporate offices, he was typically rebuked for wasting time and "acting like a child." As Jerry put it, "When I was performing for the company, I'd hear, 'Good boy'; otherwise, not a word."

But through what must have been a torturous trial-and-error procedure, Jerry discovered that by getting into gambling-related trouble—particularly with large outlays of money, his father's "life preoccupation"—he could get the attention he yearned for from this man. Jerry learned to use self-destructive gambling to incite his father's rage, which was followed by demonstrations of affection if Jerry expressed remorse and showed that he felt humiliated and defeated. Even though the attention Jerry obtained through this pattern of Pyrrhic revenge was overtly negative, it was also psychologically rewarding.

A PATHOLOGICAL WAY OF LOVING

Recall Adam, the boy described in chapter 1 who got himself expelled from New England prep schools—a maliciously intentioned pattern of self-defeat that hurt his father. Like Jerry, this boy found a way to attack his father with a pattern of Pyrrhic revenge targeted at the enterprise his father loved most—education. These examples get at the heart of this complex self-defeating dynamic: People who engage in Pyrrhic revenge learn early in life either that they are not loved in a nurturing manner or that those entrusted with the power to dispense love and affection have other priorities, such as a family business or academic excellence. Armed with this awareness, self-saboteurs can identify their targets' most sensitive concerns and use self-inflicted harm in a strategy designed to hurt whatever these flawed caregivers value most.

Many psychoanalysts interpret the actions of self-saboteurs who engage in Pyrrhic revenge as a pathological way of loving or of getting attention from people they need and are deeply involved with but also hate.[3] One prominent theory, advanced by the psychoanalyst Wilhelm Reich, maintains that these people were raised by parents who deserted or neglected them.[4] Consequently, they deeply fear confirming that they are fundamentally unloved or unworthy of attention. When events reminiscent of childhood abandonment—such as a gruff dismissal or an actual rejection by a significant person—evoke their fears, self-defeatists may use Pyrrhic-revenge tactics to establish a connectedness that wards off the terror of being alone. Simply stated: Better to be cared for enough to warrant this type of actively hostile involvement—actually, *any* involvement—than to be considered worthless and unworthy of concern.

This explanation fits uncannily with the self-destructive dynamics of both Jerry and Adam. By destroying an aspect of themselves that their fathers valued dearly—money and academic competence, respectively—these self-saboteurs generated far more attention and involvement from their fathers than they could have through appropriate achievements. Jerry's father gave perfunctory recognition to him when he was working well and ignored him on all other occasions. Similarly, Adam, the expulsion-prone student, began his Pyrrhic-revenge behavior after he returned to school from holiday visits home. If Adam could have put into words what motivated his fights when he returned to prep school, he might have said, "Dad, you hurt me terribly by kicking me out of the house. Now you'll have to come way up here and care for me after I get into trouble and have the headmaster summon you to my side."

Another related interpretation of what may have motivated Jerry to gamble himself into debt—and into his father's protective care—rests on the assumption that the inappropriate caregiving he received as a child left him caught between a proverbial rock and a hard place. On the one hand, his father's inadequate parenting generated anger and a wish for revenge. On the other, dependent children strive to maintain idealizing relationships with their parents, in part because this helps preserve the fantasy that their needs will be cared for.[5] In Jerry's case, this childhood fantasy of an idealized father was compounded by the high opinion of his father held by church officials, business and community leaders, and family friends. The problem for Jerry—and for others growing up in comparable circumstances—is that it is hard and dangerous to act aggressively toward a "saint," particularly a patron saint.

The powerlessness that results from enacting a pattern of Pyrrhic-revenge behavior is uniquely suited to achieving a compromise between staying emotionally bonded with an ambivalent love object and symbolically beating the daylights out of that object. By sabotaging healthy goal attainment or actively inflicting self-harm in ways that are immediately obvious to an ambivalently valued parent, the maliciously intentioned self-defeatist assumes a powerless status ("See, I can't hurt you") and elevates the status of the parent ("See how powerful you are"). This process is thought to provide relief to the self-defeatist by providing hope that the self-inflicted punishment will finally evoke appropriate parenting regardless of how miserably the parent has failed in the past.

VICTORY THROUGH DEFEAT

An intriguing aspect of Pyrrhic revenge is that once it evokes a desired response, this pattern gets stronger, and self-saboteurs use it even more as a weapon.[6] If, for example, the Pyrrhic-revenge tactic is "holding my breath until I turn blue," and Johnny learns that doing so will make Mommy run to him and hug him whenever he feels hurt or in need of contact, Johnny's power over Mom will climb considerably. If Mom denies him a cookie, shuts off the TV, or berates him for hitting his sister, faster than you can say "inhalation" Johnny is closemouthed, turning blue. If Mom gets wise to Johnny's manipulative intent and fails to respond, Johnny can up the ante and try fainting.

While few patterns of Pyrrhic revenge are as simple as holding your breath and turning blue, these behaviors can easily and directly influence people's behavior. Once self-defeatists know what effects their patterns of self-inflicted pain have, they can effectively use these devices in many ways.

First, these patterns can provide the psychological gratification of being able to control another person's behavior. Assume that you are accustomed to dealing with a parent who is overly critical, 90 percent of the time rebuffing what you have done. According to many behavioral psychologists, actively *provoking* the criticisms and castigations of such a parent renders the rebukes less painful by placing them under your control.[7] According to this perspective, which focuses solely on how the relief of a painful stimulus provides gratification, if punishment is expected, the anxiety of anticipating that noxious outcome is often greater than the outcome itself. In those circumstances, self-saboteurs may effectively curb their own anxiety by knowingly eliciting punishment ("Let's get it over with").

In other words, by precipitating a painful experience—that is, gaining control over when and where it will occur—maliciously intentioned self-defeatists can, paradoxically, *lessen* the degree of pain they are forced to endure.[8] According to behavioral psychologist B. F. Skinner, this is the principle that underlies confession—both the religious variety and the type seen among criminals.[9] If a person can stop a noxious stimulus, like the feeling of sinfulness or the anticipation of being punished, by bringing about the painful occurrence, the self-inflicted pain will actually prove rewarding.

A second benefit thought to be derived from Pyrrhic-revenge strategies is the reinforcement of proving a once-idealized person to be incompetent. As we saw in chapter 1 in the discussion of Mohammad Ali's "rope-a-dope" strategy, people gain certain feelings of omnipotence from being victims of ineffectiveness or abuse and rising above it.

One adolescent patient developed a remarkably powerful Pyrrhic-revenge strategy that exploited the age-old axiom of parenting that "this hurts me more than it hurts you." Stuart, the youngest of three children from a middle-class family, had what would have been diagnosed as a "conduct disorder"

according to the American Psychiatric Association's guide-
lines, except that he did not show the overtly cruel symptoms
that characterize this psychiatric disturbance.[10] Whereas conduct disorders typically involve breaking and entering, cruelty
to animals and/or people, physical fights, or forced sexual
contact, Stuart manifested none of these symptoms. Instead,
he broke whatever minor rules he could, but in a way guaranteed to be discovered by his father. For example, he would
blatantly copy from a classmate's exam and get suspended
from school; steal money from his mother's purse while his
grandmother (who lived with the family) "happened to be
watching"; or sneak drinks from his father's liquor cabinet and
leave the glass in his own bedroom. Without fail, these bungled
indiscretions would throw his father into fits of rage, and
Stuart would be violently whipped with a thick belt. In fact,
Stuart's father developed a crude justice system in which he
dispensed lashes according to the severity of Stuart's misdeed.

The interesting aspect of Stuart's pattern of crime and punishment involved what occurred following his whipping.
When Stuart had been left on his bed, sobbing and suffering
the pain of the beating, his mother would begin to castigate her
husband for being violent and for scarring Stuart's "mind and
soul." This harangue—often witnessed by Stuart, who would
leave his bed to spy on his parents if he heard his mother
screaming—would continue until his father had swallowed "at
least half a bottle of Maalox" and promised to find alternative
ways to handle his son's misbehavior. For the balance of the
evening Stuart's father would sit dejectedly in his chair, talking
to no one, "slugging down Maalox as though it were soda
pop."

Even Stuart, only sixteen years old when he entered therapy,
easily realized that his indiscretions initiated a scenario that
would ultimately punish his father. Although he could not at

first explain what the dynamics underlying his Pyrrhic-revenge strategy were, he soon recognized that he had "one up" on his father. He said: "[Dad] totally loses his cool and is then a useless wreck. I'm learning to not do bad each and every time he beats me, which means when I'm a dad, I'll be better because I learned how to act." Stuart clearly derived a sense of glory from humiliating his presumably powerful father. What remained in his psychotherapy was to help him develop self-esteem from earning legitimate kudos in place of the type achieved through the twisted logic that said "I may be bad, but I'm better than he is, which must be good."

Seeking and Rejecting Help

Pyrrhic revenge can be an effective weapon *and* esteem enhancer for "help-rejecting complainers" or in the "game" psychiatrist Eric Berne calls "Help Me If You Can . . . You Bastard."[11] This self-defeating style was first noted in psychiatric practices by therapists who felt manipulated and devalued by their patients, but it is now recognized among all maliciously intentioned self-defeatists who seek power and psychological gratification from making others fail. More specifically, in this form of Pyrrhic revenge self-saboteurs summon a caregiver (from a police officer to a priest), demonstrate a need for help, and then thwart that person's best efforts to help. Although such self-defeatists punish themselves and lose potential benefits by blocking the well-intentioned efforts of others, they gain a warped satisfaction from the realization that they have the power to render would-be caregivers (who are presumably more powerful) impotent and, at times, even embarrass and humiliate them. By enacting such a strategy of Pyrrhic revenge, people can achieve psychological victory through defeat.[12]

REPAIRING NARCISSISTIC WOUNDS THROUGH PYRRHIC REVENGE

We have not yet discussed the context within which most instances of Pyrrhic revenge take place: marriage. Among the best known of all maliciously intentioned self-saboteurs are those who initiate long-term relationships in which they regularly incite their spouses to anger or rage and then supplicate themselves before their victimized spouses and beg for forgiveness. Although the hostilities between such self-saboteurs and their spouses may become intense, such partners typically stay together even if they clearly have more favorable options.

Marie entered therapy at age twenty-nine after six years as part of what she called "the most mismatched couple on the planet." Since graduating from college, she had worked in sales development and marketing for a major firm in the computer industry, ultimately working her way up to the rank of vice-president. Marie and her husband, Alan, were childless, but she planned to have a family if she could "get the marital aspect of [her] life back on a track that resemble[d] [her] career." Marie's reported impetus for entering therapy when she did was "to break this cycle of chilled relations with Mr. Iceberg before [she] turn[ed] thirty."

As Marie said, she and Alan clearly were "night and day": she was a vivacious, beautiful extrovert, while he was a cerebral loner. Coincidentally, he was also involved in sales (for a noncompeting computer-related corporation) but was clearly inferior to his wife professionally. Marie effortlessly attracted and captivated people. Alan, while as intelligent as anyone else in his field, was not a charismatic charmer, and his sales performance reflected this shortcoming.

A pronounced difference in temperament—of a related yet distinct variety—was the source of conflict in their marriage.

Marie, who during college was elected homecoming queen and had been sexually active also, fully expected that she and Alan would sustain a healthy romantic involvement throughout their marriage. Alan, however, failed to respond to Marie affectionately or sexually despite her beauty and her expressed desires. When Marie entered therapy, she claimed that Alan had "totally lost his libido" when they had become engaged and that he was "like a eunuch." On one occasion when she prepared to greet Alan by wrapping herself in a huge ribbon— and nothing else—and lying on their living-room sofa, he walked in and asked, "What's for dinner?"

The compromise solution Marie had developed to deal with her painful feelings of rejection was a pattern of Pyrrhic revenge. Her career brought her into constant contact with men who, virtually without exception, found her extremely desirable. Marie had numerous affairs while on business trips and invariably—in a style akin to Stuart's—would leave obvious telltale evidence for Alan to find. On three occasions Marie "accidentally" let a lover have her home telephone number, and when each one called, Alan answered the phone. Marie would often fail to call Alan at prearranged times, and when he tried to locate her, she would later be unable to explain her whereabouts. On at least two occasions Marie kept the business cards of her one-night-stand partner in plain view on the desk in the home office that she and Alan shared, although the businesses represented on the cards could not possibly have related to Marie's work.

Apart from her pattern of leading Alan to these discoveries, the aspect of Marie's behavior that confirmed a diagnosis of maliciously intentioned self-defeat was the manner in which she *provocatively* confessed to having extramarital flings. When Alan would ask her, for example, "Why, when you were in Dallas, did you need to consult a stockbroker?" Marie would angrily retort, "What the hell do you care; do you think I slept with him?" Alan would say yes, and after a few more angry exchanges Marie would admit the affair, and a pitched battle would begin. He would call her "slut" or "whore," and she would respond in kind with "impotent" or "fag." After several exchanges like this lasting at least a quarter of an hour, Alan would ultimately physically abuse Marie in one way or another, prompting her to burst into tears and beg for his forgiveness. For an hour or so they would debate the pros and cons of staying together, and Alan would always forgive Marie when she promised never to "do it" again.

What followed these scenes is significant: after Marie's humiliation and apologies were complete, the couple would invariably end up having sexual relations. Their battles and Marie's anguished sobbing seemed to draw Alan out of his shell and into Marie's arms. This common scenario—often called a fight/fuck syndrome—is a form of Pyrrhic-revenge triumph that gives self-saboteurs two distinct rewards. First, they successfully control their partners by arranging to be punished, shamed, and humiliated. Second, the abusers get cornered into reaffirming the worthiness and inherent lovability of the self-saboteurs.

The psychoanalyst Robert Stolorow has described this type of maliciously intentioned self-defeating behavior as serving a narcissistic function.[13] A person with a defective sense of self can use self-defeating behaviors to form an interdependent relationship with a highly valued partner in order to acquire a sense of self-esteem. If debasing oneself in relation to another can serve to establish a symbiosis in which one is either nurtured or attended to in a desired manner, the structure of this relationship will presumably bolster, or at least temporarily maintain, the self-saboteur's sense of self-worth.

In Marie's case, psychotherapy revealed that she had very

low self-esteem despite her worldly success. An only child, Marie claimed that as far back as she could remember she had felt abandoned by her father, an aloof engineer who rarely attended to her, preferring to "tinker in the basement with his asinine inventions" or play chess with cronies. The only time she felt "noticed and worthwhile" was after age sixteen, when she reached sexual maturity and men of all ages ogled her body—a fact that helped explain why sex was so important to her. From her days as a somewhat promiscuous college student (who had even made a minor appearance in *Playboy*) to her position as an executive garnering the attention of businessmen everywhere she traveled, Marie had derived a transient sense of self-worth from her sex appeal. Yet Alan, withdrawing from her as her father had, gave her none of the reinforcement she craved—unless or until she provoked his nurturance through her Pyrrhic-revenge strategy.

In line with Stolorow's theory, psychotherapy revealed that Marie derived a double dose of self-esteem by provoking Alan to assaultive rages and, ultimately, seducing him. On the one hand, Marie achieved a victory through defeat by weathering the abuse of her aggressor/husband, whom she probably idealized subconsciously because of his resemblance to her father. On the other hand, the "turning around" of Alan's attitudes and affection—culminating in lovemaking—bolstered Marie's self-esteem. She even reported that in the aftermath of their battles she sensed that Alan "would never abandon her" as, it appears, her father had done. This hard-won bonding presumably provided Marie with the reassurance that Alan, regardless of his shortcomings, would reliably be available to her to strengthen her fragile sense of self-worth.[14]

MEA CULPA

Many psychoanalytic theories of self-defeat maintain that feelings of guilt cause patterns of Pyrrhic revenge. While it is hard to summarize the myriad theories based on the notion of guilt-induced self-defeat, they all rest on one assumption: people who provoke punishment from others either see this as the "necessary price" (to use Theodore Reik's term) for obtaining pleasure, or they seek punishment as a form of sacrifice or appeasement that will ease their guilt.[15]

What Role Does Guilt Play?

The model of guilt-induced self-defeat we see as most useful rests on the fact that many self-saboteurs experience feelings of intense, often violent or sadistic rage before they initiate behavior patterns destined to inflict pain on themselves. As Theodore Reik, the psychoanalyst who coined the term "victory through defeat," noted, often underlying such self-defeating behavior patterns is a sadistic wish to seize and destroy a person who *should* be the object of love and affection.[16] According to this perspective, the desire to conquer those who have caused you suffering, pain, and humiliation is typically fraught with guilt and fear, particularly if you are a young, dependent child. The ego therefore arranges a "psychic transformation" of this sadistic fantasy into a pattern of Pyrrhic revenge. Elegant and effective, this punitive maneuver lets self-defeatists not only express a sadistic wish but also feel less guilty about harming someone they should love.

Following this line of reasoning, we would have to conclude that Marie felt rage and aggression toward her father when he retreated to his basement workroom or to the park to play chess with his cronies. We know that Jerry experienced a desire to hurt, and we assume that most self-defeatists who engage in Pyrrhic revenge are similarly disposed to harm others. But the question is, What do we gain by agreeing that guilt can motivate this self-defeating style? We are still left with a need both to understand the basic purpose and function of this unique interaction pattern and to find a way of helping people deal with intimates more positively. Given the popularity of psychoanalytic thought, guilt is an intuitively appealing way to describe the origins of Pyrrhic revenge. But unless this concept can effectively guide psychotherapy, we prefer to ignore it and focus on the manifest drives that account for patterns of self-destructive behavior.

PYRRHIC REVENGE AND REVICTIMIZATION

In chapter 1 we expressed our concern that self-defeating behaviors not be confused with masochism. First, the term *masochism* does not accurately describe all acts of self-sabotage, and second, we do not consider so-called acts of sexual masochism to be self-defeating phenomena.[17] It is equally, if not more, important to differentiate self-defeating behaviors from a psychological disturbance best described as "revictimization."[18] Although this syndrome is thought to resemble patterns of Pyrrhic revenge, it is a distinct psychiatric disturbance, initiated and maintained by a unique set of factors. In particular, we see a need to distinguish maliciously intentioned self-defeating behaviors from instances of spouse abuse that involve women who do not leave their abusers.

In the 1980s the most notorious instance of what press reports dubbed self-destructive behavior was Hedda Nuss-

baum's relationship with Joel Steinberg, which became notorious because six-year-old Lisa Steinberg was beaten to death by
Steinberg, her (illegally) adoptive father. What made this case
particularly disturbing—and the subject of an avalanche of
media attention—was the fact that Nussbaum, a well-regarded
children's-book editor, and Steinberg, her common-law husband and an attorney, were expected to be model parents by
the social service agency that put Lisa in their care. Instead, it
was ultimately shown that Steinberg had been severely beating
both Nussbaum and their daughter for years prior to Lisa's
death.

When it was discovered that Nussbaum had endured
Steinberg's beatings and remained loyal to him—actually trying to protect him from the authorities while reconfirming
her undying love for him—the press corps reacted like
sharks in a feeding frenzy. Serving as lay psychoanalysts, they
advanced dozens of theories to explain her devotion to a
batterer and her alleged complicity in Lisa's murder. Through
it all, what weighed most heavily in favor of assuming that
Nussbaum was self-destructive was the contention that she
willingly remained with Steinberg despite opportunities to
leave him.

While Hedda Nussbaum obviously suffered some form of
psychological disturbance, we caution against concluding that
her behavior was symptomatic of a self-defeating syndrome.
Before we can confidently say that a self-saboteur is engaging
in a pattern of Pyrrhic revenge, we must first be able to
demonstrate that he or she is typically the *initiator* of the
interactive pattern of abuse or, if not, is always an equal partici-
pant. Certain behavior patterns involving battered women—
such as the Nussbaum-Steinberg one—do not pass this test.
Instead, they are better understood as being the result of
traumatic experiences, often patterns of childhood victimiza-

tion that render people susceptible to repeating the traumatiz-
ing events in adulthood. The clinical literature is replete with
case studies of such patterns.

Victims of childhood abuse who, as adults, remain in dependent relationships with those who inflict pain most often fail
to meet the criteria we have established for judging a behavior
pattern to be an instance of Pyrrhic revenge. Their tolerance
of abusive relationships is almost always a function either of
repeating a trauma, of lacking the adequate resources—such as
finances or social support—to escape their abusers, or, according to some recently advanced theories, of being "physio-
logically addicted" to receiving pain.[19] Research has shown
that regardless of the source of their dependency, victims of
uncontrollable abuse are vulnerable to revictimization in the
aftermath of trauma. This is one explanation for the finding
that childhood victims of sexual abuse are at high risk of
becoming prostitutes.[20]

No precise line can be drawn between the *symptoms* of
Pyrrhic revenge and revictimization, but some distinctions
exist. First, in the absence of evidence to the contrary, an
ongoing pattern of spouse abuse should be assumed to conform to a syndrome *other* than maliciously intentioned self-
defeat. Second, the closing phase of the behavioral sequence
should be considered carefully. Does the person experience
overt relief following the denouement, as Jerry, Stuart, or
Marie did? Or is the person more like a junkie, manifesting a
tolerance of ever-increasing "dosages" of self-inflicted pain
over time? On the surface, Nussbaum seemed to fit the latter
dynamic, so her disturbance apparently was something other
than a pattern of self-defeat.

To recap, Pyrrhic revenge may be likened to a repetition
compulsion in that the self-saboteur is trying to right a wrong,
but it goes a step further. By attempting to mask—and simul-

taneously to express—aggressive, retaliatory urges, people using this pattern of self-defeat have a powerful weapon. Like no other self-defeating syndrome that we are aware of, Pyrrhic revenge is clearly designed to achieve a psychological payback or an emotional victory through a defeat that may be costly in physical terms.

7

Resolving the Tragic Paradox

Not in the clamor of the crowded street,
Not in the shouts and plaudits of the throng,
But in ourselves, are triumph and defeat.
—W. H. Longfellow from "The Poets"

WE have now traveled from one end of the continuum of self-defeat to the other. We have seen people harm and thwart themselves in a variety of ways, in varying degrees, and for a number of distinct reasons, and we have looked closely at the numerous patterns of self-defeat. In this chapter we take a step back to look at the broad picture.

THE MYTH OF SELF-DESTRUCTIVE DRIVES

The majority of theories psychiatrists and psychologists have tried out for understanding self-defeating behavior can safely be discarded. The most important of these theories is the notion that people are innately endowed with a death wish or other motive for self-destruction, a view that Freud advanced speculatively late in his life. He thought it was theoretically elegant, which it is. He thought it fit the facts about human nature as he saw them; if it did then, it no longer does. In the thousands of pages of research we have read, and in the thousands of hours of psychotherapy and experimentation we have conducted, we have found nothing to support the view that people have a fundamental drive to defeat themselves. People do quite definitely defeat and destroy themselves, but these tragic outcomes are not intended. At most, they furnish a means to a desired end.

In general, people want to live, to succeed, to thrive, to feel good, and to enjoy good health. They do not want to fail or to suffer. When people behave self-destructively, we generally should conclude that they too hold the familiar, common wishes for health, success, and well-being. But self-saboteurs are either pursuing these wishes in a misguided, ill-advised, or dangerous way, or they are pursuing other goals that end up interfering with those normative, positive ends.

Our first conclusion, then, is that there is no inner urge toward self-destruction. This should be good news for psychotherapists, for friends and families of self-saboteurs, and even for self-defeatists themselves. After all, if self-defeat were driven by a destructive instinct, it would be virtually impossible to treat or avoid. By definition, instincts cannot be gotten rid of; at most, they can be controlled and channeled. But self-defeat is not instinctive, so hope and optimism are justified.

Our second conclusion is that there is no single cause or pattern of self-defeat. This, too, is reason to reject many previous theories, which often have taken a heavily reductionistic approach. In psychology, reductionistic theories have repeatedly been shown to be inadequate, but theorists continue to search for single explanations or one-dimensional theories despite the proven inadequacy of such approaches. Our perspective, founded on the recognition that there is no single key to explaining self-defeat, stands in stark contrast to the single-explanation perspectives that have until now dominated the literature on this subject. We have proven that people sabotage themselves in different ways and for different reasons, and these different paths to self-destruction may have little or nothing in common except the tragic endpoint. Self-defeat is not a single problem; it is a cluster or family of problems.

The goal of our work has been to demonstrate that by identifying and exploring the three dominant styles of self-defeat, this fundamental paradox becomes far more comprehensible. This approach toward establishing a three-pronged model of self-defeat seems to be the wave of the future.[1] Psychiatrists involved in framing the American Psychiatric Association's newest guide to diagnosing mental disorders plan to include among their provisional diagnoses an updated "self-defeating personality disorder" that incorporates the perspective advanced here.[2] Specifically, we propose with our model that self-destruction may be well-intentioned, self-serving, or malicious. Thus, while there are varied, nonoverlapping paths leading to self-defeat, none of them is innate or characterized by a primary or overriding goal of harming oneself.

WELL-INTENTIONED SELF-DEFEAT: BLUNDERS AND BAD BARGAINS

The most prevalent patterns of self-defeat seem to revolve around some sort of miscalculation, broadly defined to encompass poor judgment and flawed decision making. This is not surprising, since self-defeatists are guided by positive, desirable goals yet reach negative, unwanted outcomes. There are several kinds of miscalculations, and various circumstances bring them about, but the fact of miscalculation is often central to self-destruction.

In this book we have examined some of these miscalculations. One type is based on choosing a strategy that backfires: your method produces an effect opposite to what you desired. Another type of miscalculation involves making a poor bargain, so that you incur costs and risks that far exceed the value of any benefits you gained.

Going for Short-Term Gains

Although psychologists still have much to learn about these destructive miscalculations, several conclusions are already clearly established. First, many of the miscalculations that cause self-defeat are based on a narrowing of time perspective. Self-defeatists favor the short term over the long term. When the benefits are immediate and the costs will be delayed, people tend to make decisions that they will eventually regret. While it may be too strong to assert, as some have, that we are a culture of narcissists,[3] we do seem inclined toward hedonism. Like the cartoon character Popeye's friend Wimpy, who put off paying for the hamburgers he craved, we seem inclined to defer paying for what we want to consume today, regardless of the ultimate cost.

People disobey their physician's instructions because of the cost, the discomfort, the inconvenience, or simply the disagreeableness of the medicine. When the health-care provider in question is a psychotherapist, people regularly resist treatment by finding fault with the personality or behavior of the therapist, failing to attend appointments because of "real-world needs," or simply denying the need for treatment by pointing to the sickness of society as a whole. People eat unhealthy foods because those taste good. They neglect their exercise because it is too stressful or inconvenient to work out. In the short run, they benefit from these patterns, but in the long run they severely damage their health. Whenever we see a decision pattern marked by short-term gains and long-term risks and costs—whether this decision is faced by an individual, a family, or an entire nation—we should realize the substantial danger of self-destructive choices.

Seeing Only the Positive

A second pattern of miscalculation involves focusing only on the positive. People often seem to ignore or downplay the negative aspects of their choices. Clearly, this fits well with the first pattern of emphasizing short-term gains over long-term costs. Because the long-term costs are deferred, they are easy to ignore. But even if the bad outcomes are not far away, people sometimes ignore them while focusing on the positive. Gamblers typically think more about winning than about losing; if they thought more about losing, they would not enjoy gambling and would probably stop. At first blush, these errors seem like optimism or positive thinking. After all, advice books and trusted friends often advise people to look on the bright side and to regard glasses as half full rather than half empty. But such positive illusions can be dangerous.[4] Optimists who confidently assume that "it can't happen to me" sometimes learn, painfully, that bad things can indeed happen to them.

Ignoring the Probable

Yet another pattern of miscalculation involves focusing on what is definite while discounting what is merely probable.

Now most psychologists accept that people ordinarily do not make good use of statistical or probabilistic information.[5] When the benefits are definite but the costs are uncertain, people will again tend to ignore or downplay the costs, often with tragic results. As we have said, not everyone who smokes tobacco gets cancer, nor does everyone who neglects to wear a seat belt end up with brain damage from going head first through a windshield. Such costs are easy to ignore because they might never materialize. Yet they do all too often.

Making Faulty Appraisals

Further sources of misjudgment lie in people's inaccurate appraisals of themselves and their situations. People overestimate what they can accomplish or they underestimate their resources or they expect the world to treat them in certain ways if they act in certain ways. The world is less fair and less predictable than we like to think, and self-knowledge is full of gaps, inconsistencies, and myths. When people try to formulate a plan of action, they rely on their self-knowledge and their assumptions about the world, and these two bodies of misinformation are often all they have to go on. Not surprisingly, people sometimes make poor choices or end up far from where they intended to be.

Dealing with Success

Ironically, our investigation has concluded that a primary source of misjudgment is a history of being successful. Rather than yielding a clear and accurate judgment of the exigencies that can affect personal outcomes, success apparently distorts people's capacity to assess the lay of the land, particularly when interpersonal relationships are involved. We have concluded that when success is extreme or differentiates people from their peer group as being exceptional or gifted, the burdens imposed by success make people far more likely to self-destruct near or at the top than on the way there.[6]

Part of this misjudgment is uniquely American. The Horatio Alger myth that shapes a large part of our collective psyche promotes the notion that climbing the ladder to the top yields riches and rewards. What is missing from this myth—and what leads to self-destructive outcomes—is the need to integrate the goal of building interpersonal relationships with professional achievement. The failure to recognize this need for balance can yield horribly painful consequences for misguided careerists.

Handling Emotional Distress

Ignorance is not the only culprit behind self-destructive miscalculations, however. Emotion can also be involved. Over and over in this book we have seen how anxiety, sadness and depression, or other unpleasant emotional states have been intertwined into the histories of self-destruction. Sometimes, of course, emotional turmoil is a result of self-defeat, but in many cases it appears to be a cause. Emotional distress can apparently affect people's judgment processes in ways that lead to self-defeating outcomes. It is not always implicated in self-defeat (again, there is no single explanation or cause of self-destruction), but when it is present, self-defeat is more likely.

Just how does emotional distress produce self-defeat? This is perhaps the most compelling question that researchers concerned with self-defeating behavior need to address in the next few years. There are several tantalizing hints and theories, but no firm answer is available.

One likely answer is that some forms of emotional distress enhance the short-term orientation that we have identified with self-defeat. When people are angry or upset, they focus on the present even more than usual, and the long-range costs and risks associated with a given mode of action may seem especially irrelevant. Likewise, when people feel sad or depressed, the distant future may seem out of reach, and they cannot concern themselves with such long-term considerations. As a result, emotionally distraught people may make decisions that favor short-term benefits (including relief from bad feelings) despite significant long-term risks.

This tendency is so strong within the context of therapeutic relationships that psychiatric hospitals will often designate patients as being "split risks"—people likely to split, or run from the hospital grounds—when they are confronting intense emotions. The paradox here is that rather than seeking out the care of their therapist or the hospital staff during times of acute distress, many patients seek to break away from the therapeutic milieu in search of drugs, sexual escapades, or comparable escapist actions designed to relieve them from the self-focused attention demanded by psychotherapy.

Functioning as a split risk is not limited to psychiatric inpatients. The hallmark of most self-defeatists is the tendency to reject the kinds of love that nurture or help heal emotional wounds in favor of "caregiving" that results only in pain and suffering. If a passionate love affair can distract a person from confronting deep emotional wounds or psychological vulnerability, a self-defeatist often chooses such an involvement, regardless of the pain it causes.

Another explanation for the role of emotional distress in self-defeating behavior concerns a shift in how people appraise probabilities. Research has already shown that when people are experiencing pleasant emotional states, they become averse to taking risks.[7] But the converse may also be true: people who are experiencing unpleasant emotions seem more apt to take risks, a conclusion supported by ongoing research. In one recent study experimental subjects were offered a choice between two lotteries, one of which holds a high likelihood of winning a small amount, while the other is a long shot. People in unpleasant emotional states were more likely to choose the long shot, which meant their chances of losing increased dramatically. They even preferred the long shot when it was statistically a poor choice—that is, when the size of the prize was more than offset by the high chance of losing.

If emotional distress operates in this way, we can perhaps understand why: people want to escape bad feelings. This desire to escape from emotional pain may increase the tendency to focus on immediate and short-term outcomes at the expense of long-range ones. Moreover, if you are feeling bad, a small success or victory might not be enough to overcome your pain, whereas a large success would; the long shot, therefore, becomes subjectively more appealing because it represents a chance of alleviating your emotional distress. In this way, unpleasant emotions can lead people into making choices that are objectively far from optimal ones and in the end are harmful, even though they seem to make sense at the time.

SELF-SERVING SELF-DEFEAT: HATE, LOVE, AND ESCAPE

Thus far we have seen that self-defeat typically is an unwanted consequence or a side effect of miscalculations. This implies a view of the self-defeatist that differs radically from both popular stereotypes and other psychological theories.

The traditional view has been that self-destruction is rooted in some negative attitude toward the self. Self-defeat has been regarded as arising from guilt and a desire to punish oneself, from a sense of being worthless and undeserving, or from self-hatred. A few theorists (including Freud in his last years) have said that everyone holds such motives. Others have argued that only some people come to hold these negative attitudes toward the self and that they are the ones who commit self-destructive acts.

Self-love and Self-destructiveness

Our analysis provides very little to support the view that self-defeat results from a dislike of oneself. Quite the opposite, in fact: Self-defeat often seems to follow from people's inflated opinion of themselves or from an excess of narcissism.[8]

How can self-love lead to self-destruction? How does Narcissus turn into Nero? Once again, there are many answers, but they all revolve around the principle that egotism fuels irrationality. People who cling to inflated views of themselves are unwilling to face or accept negative feedback, and their efforts to avoid such feedback lead them to make the various bargains and blunders that we have found repeatedly in self-defeat. Self-handicappers refuse to confront the possibility of failure and prefer to forego success in order to preserve an illusion of competence. Overconfident people take on too much, make too many commitments and promises, and then break down under the strain. Narcissists ignore the feelings of others en route to acquiring the money and position they think can cure all ills, only to discover that only love can make the material rewards of success feel gratifying. Humiliated egotists become obsessed with revenge, and they

harm themselves in the destructive process of getting even
with whoever made them lose face.

Low Self-esteem and Self-destructiveness

To be sure, self-defeat should in principle arise from miscalculations in either direction, and we have noted some cases
in which both excessively high and excessively low self-ap-
praisals can lead to self-defeat. Self-handicapping, for example, occurs among both high- and low-self-esteem people,
although for different reasons: people with high self-esteem
handicap themselves to maximize their successes, while people with low self-esteem handicap themselves to protect
against the implications of failure.[9] In both cases, however,
the desire for a positive self-image produces self-handicapping. Likewise, we noted that people who use bargaining
strategies can suffer from either overconfidence or undercon-
fidence, but a wish to bargain successfully underlies the use
of these faulty strategies.

Thus, when self-destruction does occasionally result from
an unfavorable self-appraisal, it is not because the self-defeatists dislike themselves and wish for punishment or harm.
Rather, such people want to achieve a good outcome, but they
base their decisions on faulty information and thus sometimes
produce undesired outcomes. In an earlier chapter we used the
example of bargainers who make excessive concessions because they mistakenly believe that they are in a weak negotiat-
ing position. Such people are guided not by any wish to suffer
or lose but rather by a too-pessimistic appraisal of their bargaining strength. They differ from the majority of self-
defeatists in that their self-esteem is likely to be low rather than
high. Still, the importance of their negative self-appraisal is in

how it distorts their judgment and leads them to poor, ill-advised actions.

Concern with Others' Perceptions

A particular and important focus of egotism among self-defeatists is how others perceive them. Although the terms *egotism* and *self-esteem* refer strictly to how people evaluate themselves, it is now well established that self-defeatists are overwhelmingly concerned with how they are evaluated by others.[10] Some of the worst patterns of self-defeat are set in motion by the fear of being seen in an unflattering light by other people.

This interpersonal dimension of self-defeat was shown in many ways in the preceding chapters. Self-handicapping occurs more strongly and more frequently under public circumstances (that is, when others are watching) than in private.[11] People choke under pressure more often and more strongly when others are observing the performance; in fact, it is the burden of others' expectations, rather than of their own, that causes people to perform badly. Shy people are preoccupied with how others evaluate them, and they shun social situations partly to avoid subjecting themselves to the evaluative scrutiny of other people. Destructive persistence is more severe when people think that someone else will say, "I told you so" if they admit to an error.[12]

It is only natural to be concerned with how others perceive us, but many narcissists and egotists carry this concern to extremes. Then self-destructive patterns multiply. To persevere in a failed course of action is to court disaster, but people will apparently do that in order to prevent someone else from seeing them admit to having made a mistake.

Life-Affirming Misjudgments

In earlier chapters we discussed the stresses of high self-esteem and the resulting need to escape the self. People under such pressures do irrational things to blot out any painful awareness of their own possible deficiencies or failures, and these irrationalities may extend to alcohol and drug abuse and even suicide. Once again, though, self-defeat results not from a wish to harm or destroy the self, but simply from a wish to forget what may be substandard about the self.

As mentioned briefly in chapter 1, perhaps the most vivid recent contradiction of the stereotype of the self-loathing self-saboteur was Earvin "Magic" Johnson, the superstar basketball player who shocked the nation with the disclosure that he had contracted the AIDS virus. Johnson acknowledged that he had had sex with thousands of women during his years of eminence. If we make the reasonable assumption that he knew about AIDS yet neglected to wear condoms, then it seems appropriate to label the ruination of his health an act of self-destructive behavior. But there is not the slightest bit of evidence to suggest that he despised himself or desired to end his life; indeed, his popularity among fans, players, and the droves of women he had sex with stemmed in part from his positive, optimistic, life-affirming attitude. Even his nickname conveyed *joie de vivre*. Magic enjoyed playing basketball, living with his family, and being a star—and still does—and we may assume that he also enjoyed the prodigious promiscuity that eventually led to his undoing. One may accuse Johnson of poor judgment, excessive optimism, hedonistic pursuit of short-term pleasure, disregard for long-term risks, or irrational carelessness, but not of a drive to self-destruct.

MALICIOUSLY INTENTIONED
SELF-DEFEAT: REVENGE AT
ANY COST

The final, and most overtly disordered, self-defeating style we have identified is also the most interpersonal of the three. To achieve Pyrrhic revenge, self-defeatists hurt themselves and their intimate partners with the same gesture. In fact, people who use maliciously intentioned patterns of self-defeat exploit the existence of intimate emotional ties to achieve one of their goals: the symbolic righting of a wrong (or pattern of wrong-doing) they suffered during childhood.

While we have debunked the notion that self-defeatists derive pleasure from punishment, it is hard to argue that Pyrrhic revenge is not a pathological way of receiving love. Because people who exhibit this self-defeating style are the products of parents who loved them in pathological ways, their adult love relationships tend to pattern the interactive styles they know best: verbal or physical abuse, desertion, abandonment, a combination of idealization and devaluation, and the like. Yet beneath these pathological ways of loving lies the second fundamental goal of the maliciously intentioned self-defeatist: the establishment of an interpersonal bond that wards off the terror of being alone.

We have found that self-defeatists who employ Pyrrhic revenge in relationships are, like all other self-defeatists, also centrally concerned with shoring up a potentially defective sense of self. Yet in contrast to other self-defeatists who manipulate aspects of the self in pursuit of self-esteem protection, the maliciously intentioned self-defeatist derives self-enhancement by establishing interdependence with a highly valued partner. This symbiosis, though painful and punishing on the surface, provides a structure that can nurture or bolster the self-saboteur's sense of self-worth. As long as the link with the partner is maintained—whether through repetitive shouting matches, fights, or oscillating separations and reunions— the Pyrrhic-revenge seeker feels relief from a gnawing sense of emptiness or self-loathing by being linked with the valued partner.

Pyrrhic revenge is the self-defeating style most likely to be misapplied as a term in clinical diagnosis since it fits, on the surface at least, antiquated notions of the way masochists functioned: as helpless, clinging females who derived pleasure by being dominated by more powerful males. Nothing, it turns out, could be farther from the truth. The hallmark of Pyrrhic-revenge seekers is that they are in control of their suffering, orchestrating virtually every aspect of the relationship used to give them a sense of belonging. By regularly initiating and then terminating the noxious battles they engage in with abusing partners, these self-defeatists gain an added sense of self-efficacy. Controlling the actions of idealized partners—regardless of how punishing they may be on the surface—renders the world a more manageable, safer place.

The question, of course, is why these people cannot love or be loved in so-called normal ways. Why are caring lovers rejected as uninteresting, unstimulating, and the like? Why, too, are those who engage in Pyrrhic revenge so reluctant to be extricated from abusive relationships? Their failure to assess adequately the reward possibilities open in their environment goes well beyond the errors in reasoning that other self-defeatists make. Because of this ostensible irrationality, their actions perpetuate the fallacy that some self-defeatists are driven by demonic traits toward a destiny of despair. In fact, these individuals are grappling ineffectually to resolve the effects of traumas that left them yearning for those entrusted with their emotional health and well-being to act appropriately.

Although their repetitive involvements with parent substitutes cannot resolve the scars left by abusive parenting, it is possible to help the Pyrrhic-revenge seeker—and all other self-defeatists for that matter—if they are helped to understand what impels them toward their self-destructive ends.

PREVENTING SELF-DEFEAT

This book is not intended as a blueprint for psychotherapy or self-help. Still, it seems worthwhile to spend a few moments summarizing how our analysis points toward implications for minimizing self-defeat. Our remarks are not aimed at saying precisely how self-defeat can be precluded or minimized, but rather at indicating what would need to be achieved—what mechanisms would have to be reversed—for that to occur.

Carefully Making Judgments

We have shown that many instances of self-defeat result from miscalculations (broadly defined). One potential remedy for self-defeat, then, would involve adjusting your thinking to avoid the errors and biases that produce such misjudgments. Simply being aware of the standard patterns of destructive misjudgment may be a significant help toward avoiding them. Thus, if you recognize that there is a pervasive tendency to make bad judgments by ignoring long-term risks and costs, you may be able to avoid self-destruction by paying extra attention to such long-range factors while making decisions. Likewise, we concluded that destructive miscalculations often involve focusing on the definite while ignoring the merely possible, so a corrective procedure would be to consider the possible outcomes carefully, along with their implications.

Another cause of self-defeat is emotional distress. Unpleasant emotional states are not going to disappear any more than egotism is, and the most promising strategy would seem to be to learn to control them. The key is to learn how these emotions produce the misjudgments and irrationalities that bring self-destruction. As we have noted, this is a leading challenge for the next generation of researchers who must determine how emotional states affect thinking processes. In the meantime, the best you can do is to recognize that self-defeat becomes more likely when you are feeling down and to learn either to reduce such states or to minimize their consequences. At least, you can try to avoid making decisions or commitments while feeling bad emotions.

We have argued that egotism contributes to many of the irrational choices that lead to destructive consequences. Perhaps these harmful consequences can be diminished by simply admitting to having made a mistake or failed. This is a tactic that few people are willing to engage in for fear of repercussion. But admissions of human frailty, feet of clay, or circumscribed shortcomings have rarely engendered dire consequences.

Instead of striving like a workaholic to avoid looking inept, you might risk tarnishing your image by exposing an Achilles heel and discovering in fact that you are valued as a person, not just a producer. Instead of handicapping yourself by refusing to compete, you might accept the risk of failure and make an honest effort to succeed. Instead of dwelling on costly plots to avenge a slight insult or loss of face, you can try to dismiss the incident and move on to more constructive endeavors. The problem is that humility and self-acceptance are incredibly hard to come by. Our culture is not only founded on myths that foster the belief that climbing to the top will bring all the rewards life has to offer but sustained by a competitive individualism that is intolerant of second-place finishers or also-rans. Before people will be able to feel safe in admitting frailty and flaws, they must first realize that more than competence underlies psychological satisfaction.

Finding Substitute Benefits

A second approach to controlling self-defeat can be built on our analysis of destructive trade-offs. In a trade-off, the person obtains some benefits while incurring costs and risks. To avoid self-defeat, the person must find some other way to attain those benefits—or learn to live without them. Therapists, family members, and others who must deal with a self-saboteur must analyze what benefit that person derives from his or her actions and then propose a substitute. If, for example, it was determined that a self-sabotaging student misbehaved in school to secure the attention of inattentive parents (a process known in psychiatry as securing "secondary gain"), the only way to address the disorder would be for the parents to withhold attention while disciplining their child and to provide it actively after healthful behaviors. For example, if the young self-defeatist's parents were called to school because their child misbehaved, they might bring the child home in silence, provide a written description of the punishment they've decided upon, and inform the child that she or he can talk again with the family at evening dinner. Only at that time should the parents engage in conversation. This simple strategy of withdrawing desired outcomes derived from self-defeating actions, and providing them for behaviors that are healthful, can effectively eliminate the vast majority of destructive trade-offs children use to shape parents' interactive styles.

Accepting Imperfections

Finally, when considering maliciously intentioned patterns of self-defeat, it is important to help the self-defeatist recognize that all battles cannot be won and that all it takes is one healthy win to feel loved. If you can live without retribution, if you know the contributions that others have made to failed relationships, and if you are content to realize that some losses are unjustified, life is far more livable. We do not, despite the protestations of many of our leaders, live in a meritocracy, and the world is not always just. Being resigned to these external imperfections—as well as to personal ones—will often reduce the pressures that drive many self-defeatists to engineer their own demise.

Accepting Criticism

Patterns of self-defeat derived from an excessive concern with the self are more difficult to manage, but they can be treated. The primary approach is to let self-handicappers know that most people share their concerns about competency. In essence, we are, as adults, all still a bunch of kids running around a schoolyard at recess, hoping that we will not be ostracized, rejected from group activities or embarrassed when called on to perform. Once self-defeatists feel comfortable with this insight, the next step is to erase the "if someone else wins, I lose" mentality that so many people bring to social interactions.

This competitive mentality also poisons intimate relationships and can arguably be seen as the causal agent most often responsible for derailing the self-defeatist's involvement in psychotherapy. The most difficult task confronting self-defeatists is to shift the focus from other people's flaws to their own. For many self-defeatists, the most effective approach is couples therapy, which enables the therapist to point out the problem of each partner in the presence of the other. Beginning therapy with the notion, "To the jackass over there, you are the 'jackass over there,' " is often an effective means of disarming a self-defeatist's tendency to ignore personal flaws at all costs. At a minimum, this maxim helps the self-defeatist confront the utter futility of striving to shield the self from any and all forms of criticism and debasement.

Fostering a tolerance of self-deprecation is particularly important for self-handicappers, who are often striving to adhere to performance standards well beyond their reach. A well-intentioned, but horribly disruptive, approach to their concerns is to try to boost their egos with support and encouragement.[13] In essence, this is like throwing gasoline on a fire. Attempting to help self-defeatists who fear failure perform better only heightens their potential for losing. A more constructive approach is to help such people disengage from the pursuit of success, which enables them to begin accepting themselves for who they are, not for what they do.

When this approach fails, it is often effective to demonstrate that many people who are highly valued by society tolerate their defects with both humor and equanimity. Fostering a self-deprecatory style is not only an effective way for self-defeatists to begin approaching their shortcomings but, because it is actually a variant of many self-defeating styles, is often quite a comfortable way. Remember, if you present your worst features to those who may condemn you for them (like

the celebrity weatherman Willard Scott, who regularly adver-
tises his bald head or excess weight on television), you effectively take the wind out of their often hostile sails.

CONCLUDING THOUGHTS

Many great thinkers and spiritual leaders have observed that
suffering is part of the human condition, and although the
degree of suffering may change, the fact of suffering appears to
be permanent. All human beings are at the mercy of natural
and social forces far bigger than themselves, and this profound
vulnerability means that some suffering is inevitable. When
Freud, in one of his most compelling works, analyzed the
prospects for human happiness, he noted that there are many
causes of unhappiness both within and outside of the individual, and he concluded that neither nature nor culture seems
geared to increase human happiness.[14]

But there is no reason to give up simply because life seems
to guarantee at least a certain minimal amount of suffering
—on the contrary, that is all the more reason to exert ourselves to keep suffering to that minimum. And in this connection, self-defeating behavior becomes a prime target for concern and for change. Even if we cannot stop crime, aging,
disease, and people's inhumanity to others, we can at least try
to avoid being our own worst enemies.

We must also recognize that the surest cure for the narcissism and egoistic concerns that drive some of the most maladaptive patterns of self-defeat can only be achieved by getting
involved with others. Although the best remedy for pathological self-love is forming a union with one other person, commitment to social causes that foster humanitarian—rather
than self-promotional—interests will do almost as well. If the

forming of spiritual involvements and adult love relationships is not the ultimate answer, it is the penultimate resolution of the concerns underlying many patterns of self-defeat.

In this book we have described various patterns of self-defeat, and we have made a few suggestions and observations about how such patterns might be reduced or minimized. These suggestions will not bring any immediate or magical solution to the problems of self-defeat. Indeed, we doubt that such a solution is even possible. The causes of self-defeat are deeply rooted in human development and cultural conditioning. But the ineluctable first step toward ending self-defeat is unmistakable: understanding. We have tried in this book to increase the collective understanding of how people become their own worst enemies. We hope that this understanding will provide a viable foundation for constructive efforts to resolve the tragic paradox of self-defeat and to help people live more contentedly with themselves.

Living happily ever after may be confined to fantasies and fairy tales. There are too many destructive forces in the world to leave any room for hope that people will one day be able to live without suffering. The most controllable of those destructive forces, however, is the self. If human beings could eventually learn to stop their self-destructive ways of acting, then there would be one less enemy to contend with in the world, one less major cause of human suffering. That hope justifies renewed efforts to understand and deal with the tragic paradox of self-defeat.

Notes

Chapter 1:
Snatching Defeat from the Jaws of Victory

1. P. Hoban, "Prodigal Son: After the Drug Bust, Eugene Fodor Tries a Comeback," *New York,* Dec. 4, 1989, p. 100.
2. This example was taken from S. Berglas, "Self-handicapping and Self-handicappers: A Cognitive/Attributional Model of Interpersonal Self-protective Behavior," in *Perspectives in Personality,* vol. 1, ed. R. Hogan and W. H. Jones (Greenwich, Conn.: JAI Press, 1985), pp. 235–70.
3. S. Freud, "Beyond the Pleasure Principle," in *The Standard Edition of the Complete Psychological Works of Sigmund Freud,* vol. 18, ed. J. Strachey (London: Hogarth Press, 1981), p. 7; original work published in 1920.
4. For example, R. J. Ringer, *Winning through Intimidation* (Greenwich, Conn.: Fawcett Crest Books, 1973).
5. J. N. Baker and H. Manly, "Mississippi Gothic," *Newsweek,* Oct. 8, 1990, p. 36.
6. Ibid.
7. See the cover of *Newsweek,* May 18, 1987, and M. Kramer, "The Self-destruction of Gary Hart," *U.S. News and World Report,* May 18, 1987, p. 25.
8. R. F. Baumeister, *Escaping the Self: Alcoholism, Spirituality, Masochism, and Other Flights from the Burden of Selfhood* (New York: Basic Books, 1991).
9. R. V. Kraft-Ebing, *Psychopathia Sexualis: A Medico-Forensic Study* (New York: Pioneer Publications, 1950); original work published in 1901.
10. G. Fulcher, "A Review of Self-injurious Behavior—(SIB)," *Australia and New Zealand Journal of Developmental Disabilities* 10 (1984): 51–67.

11. S. Freud, "The Economic Problem in Masochism," in *The Standard Edition of the Complete Psychological Works of Sigmund Freud,* vol. 19, ed. J. Strachey (London: Hogarth Press, 1981), pp. 159–70; original work published in 1924.

12. Ibid.

13. Ibid., pp. 7–64.

14. Ibid.

15. S. Freud, "A Child Is Being Beaten. A Contribution to the Study of the Origin of Sexual Perversions," in *Collected Papers,* vol. 2, ed. E. Jones (New York: Basic Books, 1959), pp. 172–201; original work published in 1919.

16. O. Fenichel, *The Psychoanalytic Theory of Neurosis* (New York: Norton, 1954).

17. S. Freud, "Beyond the Pleasure Principle," pp. 7–64.

18. B. A. van der Kolk, "The Compulsion to Repeat the Trauma: Re-enactment, Revictimization, and Masochism," *Psychiatric Clinics of North America* 12 (1989): 389–411.

19. R. F. Baumeister and S. J. Scher, "Self-defeating Behavior Patterns among Normal Individuals: Review and Analysis of Common Self-destructive Tendencies," *Psychological Bulletin* 104 (1988): 3–22.

20. J. G. Hull, "A Self-awareness Model of the Causes and Effects of Alcohol Consumption," *Journal of Abnormal Psychology* 90 (1981): 586–600.

21. S. Duval and R. A. Wicklund, *A Theory of Objective Self-awareness* (New York: Academic Press, 1972).

22. J. G. Hull and R. D. Young, "Self-consciousness, Self-esteem, and Success-failure as Determinants of Alcohol Consumption in Male Social Drinkers," *Journal of Personality and Social Psychology* 44 (1983): 1097–1109.

23. R. L. Higgins, C. R. Snyder, and S. Berglas, *Self-Handicapping: The Paradox That Isn't* (New York: Plenum, 1990).

24. See R. C. Simons, "Psychoanalytic Contributions to Psychiatric Nosology: Forms of Masochistic Behavior," *Journal of the American Psychoanalytic Association* 35 (1987): 583–608, the source of this example and of an insightful psychoanalytic perspective on self-defeating behaviors.

25. R. Lowenstein, "A Contribution to the Psychoanalytic Theory of Masochism," *Journal of the American Psychoanalytic Association* 32 (1957): 325–56.

26. T. Reik, *Masochism in Modern Man* (New York: Farrar and Rinehart, 1941).

27. J. Haley, *The Power Tactics of Jesus Christ* (New York: Avon Books, 1969).

Chapter 2:
When Good Intentions Backfire

1. See S. Berglas, *The Success Syndrome* (New York: Plenum, 1986), on career devastation.
2. M. McMillian, "Car Caper: Reach Out and Bust Someone," *Cleveland Plain Dealer,* Dec. 30, 1990, pp. 1-A, 4-A.
3. R. F. Baumeister and S. J. Scher, "Self-defeating Behavior Patterns among Normal Individuals: Review and Analysis of Common Self-destructive Tendencies," *Psychological Bulletin* 104 (1988): 3–22.
4. Berglas, *Success Syndrome.*
5. This is according to F. McNulty, *The Burning Bed* (New York: Harcourt Brace Jovanovich, 1980).
6. D. B. McFarlin, "Persistence in the Face of Failure; The Impact of Self-esteem and Contingency Information," *Personality and Social Psychology Bulletin* 11 (1985): 153–63.
7. Many studies have found this. See, for example, J. S. Shrauger and P. B. Sorman, "Self-evaluations, Initial Success and Failure, and Improvement as Determinants of Persistence," *Journal of Consulting and Clinical Psychology* 45 (1977): 784–95. For a review of the self-esteem literature, see R. F. Baumeister, ed., *Self-Esteem: The Puzzle of Low Self-Regard* (New York: Plenum, 1993).
8. D. B. McFarlin, R. F. Baumeister, and J. Blascovich, "On Knowing When to Quit: Task Failure, Self-esteem, Advice, and Nonproductive Persistence," *Journal of Personality* 52 (1984): 138–55.
9. McFarlin, "Persistence in the Face of Failure."
10. *Wall Street Journal,* May 13, 1992, pp. A1, A9.
11. S. Freud, "The Economic Problem in Masochism," in *The Standard Edition of the Complete Psychological Works of Sigmund Freud,* vol. 21, ed. J. Strachey (London: Hogarth Press, 1981), pp. 159–70; original work published in 1924. For additional psychoanalytic perspectives, see K. Horney, "The Problem of the Negative Therapeutic Reaction," *Psychoanalytic Quarterly* 5 (1936): 29–44.
12. For a review of this literature, see B. A. van der Kolk, "The Compulsion to Repeat the Trauma: Reenactment, Revictimization, and Masochism," *Psychiatric Clinics of North America* 12 (1989): 389–411.
13. Ibid.
14. Berglas, *Success Syndrome.*
15. S. Berglas, "Horatio Alger and the Mid-Life Crisis," *New York Times,* Aug. 11, 1991, Business Section, p. 14.

16. B. M. Staw, "Knee-deep in the Big Muddy: A Study of Escalating Commitment to a Chosen Course of Action," *Organizational Behavior and Human Performance* 16 (1976): 27–44. For a review of this literature, see Baumeister and Scher, "Self-defeating Behavior Patterns"; and A. I. Teger, *Too Much Invested to Quit* (New York: Pergamon, 1980).

17. J. Z. Rubin and J. Brockner, "Factors Affecting Entrapment in Waiting Situations: The Rosencrantz and Guildenstern Effect," *Journal of Personality and Social Psychology* 31 (1975): 1054–63.

18. M. H. Bazerman, T. Giuliano, and A. Appelman, "Escalation of Commitment in Individual and Group Decision Making," *Organizational Behavior and Human Performance* 33 (1984): 141–52.

19. F. V. Fox and B. M. Staw, "The Trapped Administrator: Effects of Insecurity and Policy Resistance upon Commitment to a Course of Action," *Administrative Sciences Quarterly* 24 (1979): 449–71.

20. J. Brockner, J. Z. Rubin, and E. Lang, "Face-saving and Entrapment," *Journal of Experimental Social Psychology* 17 (1981): 68–79. See also S. Berglas and E. E. Jones, "Drug Choice as a Self-handicapping Strategy in Response to Non-contingent Success," *Journal of Personality and Social Psychology* 36 (1978): 405–17; E. E. Jones and S. C. Berglas, "Control of Attributions about the Self through Self-handicapping Strategies: The Appeal of Alcohol and the Role of Underachievement," *Personality and Social Psychology Bulletin* 4 (1978): 200–206; and S. Berglas, *Success Syndrome.*

21. E. J. Conlon and G. Wolf, "The Moderating Effects of Strategy, Visibility, and Involvement on Allocation Behavior: An Extension of Staw's Escalation Paradigm," *Organizational Behavior and Human Performance* 26 (1980): 172–92.

22. American Psychiatric Association, *Diagnostic and Statistical Manual of Mental Disorders,* 3rd ed., rev. (Washington, D.C.: Author, 1987). See also, for example, J. C. Perry and R. B. Flannery, "Passive Aggressive Personality Disorder: Treatment Implications of a Clinical Typology," *Journal of Nervous and Mental Disease* 170 (1982): 164–73.

23. J. Brockner, M. C. Shaw, and J. Z. Rubin, "Factors Affecting Withdrawal from an Escalating Conflict: Quitting before It's Too Late," *Journal of Experimental Social Psychology* 15 (1979): 492–503.

24. For examples and discussion, see Berglas, *Success Syndrome.*

25. L. B. Rubin, *Worlds of Pain: Life in the Working-Class Family* (New York: Basic Books, 1976).

26. For a discussion of some of the particular problems of this group, see Berglas, *Success Syndrome.*

27. See Rubin, *Worlds of Pain.*

28. Of course, other factors may enter into such problems as well; see Berglas, *Success Syndrome.*

29. F. McNulty, *Burning Bed,* p. 299.

30. See R. F. Baumeister, "The Optimal Margin of Illusion," *Journal of Social and Clinical Psychology* 8 (1989): 176–89.

31. S. E. Taylor, *Positive Illusions: Creative Self-deception and the Healthy Mind* (New York: Basic Books, 1989); also S. E. Taylor and J. D. Brown, "Illusion and Well-Being: A Social Psychological Perspective on Mental Health," *Psychological Bulletin* 103 (1988): 193–210.

32. See, for example, P. M. Gollwitzer and R. F. Kinney, "Effects of Deliberative and Implemental Mindsets on Illusion of Control," *Journal of Personality and Social Psychology* 56 (1989): 531–42.

33. L. S. Perloff and B. K. Fetzer, "Self–Other Judgments and Perceived Vulnerability to Victimization," *Journal of Personality and Social Psychology* 50 (1986): 502–10.

34. J. M. Burger and L. Burns, "The Illusion of Unique Invulnerability and the Use of Effective Contraception," *Personality and Social Psychology Bulletin* 14 (1988): 264–70.

35. Ibid.

36. R. Shilts, *And the Band Played On: Politics, People, and the AIDS Epidemic* (New York: Viking Penguin, 1987).

37. Ibid.

38. Berglas, *Success Syndrome.*

39. B. Shaw, "Effect of Johnson's Announcement Wearing Off," *Cleveland Plain Dealer,* Feb. 2, 1992, p. 11-D.

40. Ibid.

41. S. Schama, *Citizens: A Chronicle of the French Revolution* (New York: Vintage Random House, 1989).

42. M. E. P. Seligman, *Helplessness: On Depression, Development, and Death* (San Francisco: Freeman, 1975).

43. J. B. Overmier and M. E. P. Seligman, "Effects of Inescapable Shock upon Subsequent Escape and Avoidance Learning," *Journal of Comparative and Physiological Psychology* 63 (1967): 23–33.

44. See, for example, S. Roth and R. R. Bootzin, "Effects of Experimentally Induced Expectancies of External Control: An Investigation of Learned Helplessness," *Journal of Personality and Social Psychology* 29 (1974): 253–64.

45. See, for example, S. Roth and L. Kubal, "Effects of Noncontingent Reinforcement on Tasks of Differing Importance: Facilitation and Learned Helplessness," *Journal of Personality and Social Psychology* 32 (1975): 680–91.

46. Noncontingent success also can cause problems that are not entirely different. See Berglas and Jones, "Drug Choice as a Self-handicapping Strategy"; Jones and Berglas, "Control of Attributions"; and Berglas, *Success Syndrome.*

47. See, for example, J. Crocker and B. Major, "Social Stigma and Self-esteem: The Self-protective Properties of Stigma," *Psychological Review* 96 (1989): 608–30.

48. J. Rodin and E. Langer, "Long-term Effects of a Control-Relevant Intervention with the Institutionalized Aged," *Journal of Personality and Social Psychology* 35 (1977): 897–902.

49. L. Y. Abramson, M. E. P. Seligman, and J. D. Teasdale, "Learned Helplessness in Humans: Critique and Reformulation," *Journal of Abnormal Psychology* 87 (1978): 49–74.

50. C. S. Carver, P. H. Blaney, and M. F. Scheier, "Reassertion and Giving Up: The Interactive Role of Self-Directed Attention and the Outcome Expectancy," *Journal of Personality and Social Psychology* 37 (1979): 1859–70.

51. E. E. Jones and C. Wortman, *Ingratiation: An Attributional Approach* (Morristown, N.J.: General Learning Press, 1973).

52. E. E. Jones, K. J. Gergen, and R. G. Jones, "Tactics of Ingratiation among Leaders and Subordinates in a Status Hierarchy," *Psychological Monographs* 77 (1963): whole no. 566.

53. See J. W. Brehm and A. Cole, "Effect of a Favor Which Reduces Freedom," *Journal of Personality and Social Psychology* 3 (1966): 420–26.

54. M. H. Bazerman, *Human Judgement in Managerial Decision Making* (New York: Wiley, 1986); M. H. Bazerman, "Why Negotiations Go Wrong," *Psychology Today* 20 (1986): 54–58.

55. D. G. Pruitt, *Negotiation Behavior* (New York: Academic Press, 1981); D. G. Pruitt and J. Z. Rubin, *Social Conflict: Escalation, Stalemate, and Settlement* (New York: Random House, 1984).

56. M. Neale and M. H. Bazerman, "Systematic Deviations from Rationality in Negotiator Behavior: The Framing of Conflict and Negotiator Overconfidence," *Academy of Management Journal* 28 (1985): 34–49.

57. See Baumeister and Scher, "Self-defeating Behavior Patterns."

58. Bazerman, *Human Judgement.*

Chapter 3:
Choking under Pressure

1. See S. Berglas, *The Success Syndrome* (New York: Plenum, 1986), on pressures of success.
2. R. F. Baumeister, "Choking under Pressure: Self-consciousness and Paradoxical Effects of Incentives on Performance," *Journal of Personality and Social Psychology* 46 (1984): 610–20.
3. Ibid.
4. R. F. Baumeister and C. J. Showers, "A Review of Paradoxical Performance Effects: Choking under Pressure in Sports and Mental Tests," *European Journal of Social Psychology* 16 (1986): 361–83.
5. See G. Kimble and L. Perlmuter, "The Problem of Volition," *Psychological Review* 77 (1970): 361–84.
6. See, for example, S. Duval and R. A. Wicklund, *A Theory of Objective Self-awareness* (New York: Academic Press, 1972); R. A. Wicklund, "Objective Self-awareness," in *Advances in Experimental Social Psychology*, vol. 8, ed. L. Berkowitz (New York: Academic Press, 1975), pp. 233–75; and C. S. and Carver and M. F. Scheier, *Attention and Self-regulation: A Control-Theory Approach to Human Behavior* (New York: Springer-Verlag, 1981).
7. R. F. Baumeister, D. G. Hutton, and K. J. Cairns, "Negative Effects of Praise on Skilled Performance," *Basic and Applied Social Psychology* 1 (1990): 131–48.
8. See Berglas, *Success Syndrome*.
9. S. Freud, "Some Character Types Met in Psychoanalytic Work," in *Collected Papers*, vol. 4, ed. E. Jones (New York: Basic Books, 1949), pp. 318–44.
10. See K. Horney, "The Problem of the Negative Therapeutic Reaction," *Psychoanalytic Quarterly* 5 (1936): 29–44.
11. Berglas, *Success Syndrome*.
12. J. S. House, "Occupational Stress and Coronary Heart Disease: A Review and Theoretical Integration," *Journal of Health and Social Behavior* 15 (1974): 12–27; Berglas, *Success Syndrome*.
13. B. R. Schlenker and M. R. Leary, "Social Anxiety and Self-preservation: A Conceptualization and Model," *Psychological Bulletin* 92 (1982): 641–69.
14. They did not count the ten World Series in which the same team won all the games; these were deemed mismatches. If one team is much

better than the other, then factors like home field and choking should not make much difference. And, indeed, among those ten "sweeps," the home field was irrelevant. For a discussion of related research, see R. F. Baumeister and A. Steinhilber, "Paradoxical Effects of Supportive Audiences on Performance under Pressure: The Home Field Disadvantage in Sports Championships," *Journal of Personality and Social Psychology* 47 (1984): 85–93.

15. This parallels the irony of the success syndrome, in which success brings the sort of suffering normally associated more with failure; see Berglas, *Success Syndrome*.

16. J. Diaz, "Perils of Putting," *Sports Illustrated*, Apr. 3, 1989, pp. 76–79.

17. Ibid., p. 79.

18. Baumeister and Steinhilber, "Paradoxical Effects." Again, the researchers deleted all series that were four-game sweeps. It is noteworthy that the NBA has many playoff levels, and the early rounds of the playoffs pit the best teams against the worst, so one should expect the superior teams—who typically play more games at home because of the scheduling rules—to win most of the games. The tendency to choke should probably be anticipated only in the final round, when identity fulfillment is at stake.

A further implication of the identity-fulfillment hypothesis is that defending champions should be less prone to choke than first-time champions, and this represents a problem for using the NBA data, for the dynasties in that league have been especially striking. Baumeister and Steinhilber chose to begin the survey in 1967 because that came after a decade of solid dominance by the Boston Celtics. During that period, indeed, any home-field advantage seemed to mean little, for Boston simply always won. Likewise, the supremacy enjoyed by the Los Angeles Lakers in the 1980s, particularly in their conference, probably minimized any tendency for the data to show an effect of home field or choking.

19. More generally, there are individual differences in all sorts of problems associated with success; see J. O. Cavenar, Jr., and D. S. Werman, "Origins of the Fear of Success," *American Journal of Psychiatry* 138 (1981): 95–98.

20. D. M. Tice, J. Buder, and R. F. Baumeister, "Development of Self-consciousness: At What Age Does Audience Pressure Disrupt Performance?" *Adolescence* 20 (1985): 301–5.

21. Fluctuation is measured by item variance; see R. F. Baumeister and D. M. Tice, "Metatraits," *Journal of Personality* 56 (1988): 571–98.

Chapter 4:
Trade-offs

1. S. Berglas, *The Success Syndrome* (New York: Plenum, 1986). See also E. E. Jones and S. Berglas, "Control of Attributions about the Self through Self-handicapping Strategies: The Appeal of Alcohol and the Role of Underachievement," *Personality and Social Psychology Bulletin* 4 (1978): 200–206.

2. R. F. Baumeister and S. J. Scher, "Self-defeating Behavior Patterns among Normal Individuals: Review and Analysis of Common Self-destructive Tendencies," *Psychological Bulletin* 104 (1988): 3–22.

3. Berglas, *Success Syndrome*. See also S. Berglas and E. E. Jones, "Drug Choice as a Self-handicapping Strategy in Response to Non-contingent Success," *Journal of Personality and Social Psychology* 36 (1978): 405–17; and Jones and Berglas, "Control of Attributions."

4. B. Silverstein, "Cigarette Smoking, Nicotine Addiction, and Relaxation," *Journal of Personality and Social Psychology* 42 (1982): 946–50.

5. See R. F. Baumeister, "Masochism as Escape from Self," *Journal of Sex Research* 25 (1988): 28–59; R. F. Baumeister, *Masochism and the Self* (Hillsdale, N.J.: Erlbaum, 1989); R. F. Baumeister, "Suicide as Escape from Self," *Psychological Review* 97 (1990): 90–113; and R. F. Baumeister, *Escaping the Self: Alcoholism, Spirituality, Masochism, and Other Flights from the Burden of Selfhood* (New York: Basic Books, 1991).

6. J. G. Hull, "A Self-awareness Model of the Causes and Effects of Alcohol Consumption," *Journal of Abnormal Psychology* 90 (1981): 586–600.

7. R. A. Wicklund, "Objective Self-awareness," in *Advances in Experimental Social Psychology,* vol. 8, ed. L. Berkowitz (New York: Academic Press, 1975).

8. See Berglas and Jones, "Drug Choice as a Self-handicapping Strategy"; Jones and Berglas, "Control of Attributions"; and Berglas, *Success Syndrome*.

9. Berglas, *Success Syndrome*.

10. J. M. Dunbar and A. J. Stunkard, "Adherence to Diet and Drug Regimen," in *Nutrition, Lipids, and Coronary Heart Disease,* ed. R. Levy,

B. Fifkind, B. Dennis, and N. Ernst (New York: Raven Press, 1979), pp. 391–423.

11. D. L. Sackett and J. C. Snow, "The Magnitude of Compliance and Noncompliance," in *Compliance in Health Care*, ed. R. B. Haynes, D. W. Taylor, and D. L. Sackett (Baltimore: Johns Hopkins University Press, 1979), pp. 11–22.

12. See Baumeister and Scher, "Self-defeating Behavior Patterns," for a review of the literature on this topic and for extensive references.

13. Ibid.

14. C. Shepherd, "News of the Weird," *Cleveland Plain Dealer Magazine,* Dec. 16, 1990, p. 4.

15. B. R. Brown and H. Garland, "The Effects of Incompetency, Audience Acquaintanceship, and Anticipated Evaluative Feedback on Face-saving Behavior," *Journal of Experimental Social Psychology* 7 (1971): 490–502. See also R. F. Baumeister and J. Cooper, "Can the Public Expectation of Emotion Cause That Emotion?" *Journal of Personality* 49 (1980): 49–59; and Berglas, *Success Syndrome*.

16. B. W. Tuchman, *The March of Folly: From Troy to Vietnam* (New York: Ballantine, 1984).

17. B. R. Brown, "The Effects of Need to Maintain Face on Interpersonal Bargaining," *Journal of Experimental Social Psychology* 4 (1968): 107–22.

18. S. Jacoby, *Wild Justice: The Evolution of Revenge* (New York: Harper and Row, 1983).

19. See P. Zimbardo. *Shyness: What It Is, What to Do about It* (New York: Jove, 1987).

20. A. H. Buss, *Self-consciousness and Social Anxiety* (San Francisco: Freeman, 1980); M. R. Leary, "Affective and Behavioral Consequences of Shyness: Implications for Theory, Measurement, and Research," in *Shyness: Perspectives on Research and Treatment*, ed. W. H. Jones, J. M. Cheek, & S. R. Briggs (New York: Plenum, 1986).

21. B. R. Schlenker and M. R. Leary, "Social Anxiety and Self-presentation: A Conceptualization and Model," *Psychological Bulletin* 92 (1982): 641–69. For another perspective, see Jones and Berglas, "Control of Attributions."

22. For a review of the literature, see Baumeister and Scher, "Self-defeating Behavior Patterns."

Chapter 5:
Self-handicapping

1. R. L. Higgins, C. R. Snyder, and S. Berglas, *Self-handicapping: The Paradox That Isn't* (New York: Plenum, 1990).
2. S. Berglas and E. E. Jones, "Drug Choice as a Self-handicapping Strategy in Response to Noncontingent Success," *Journal of Personality and Social Psychology* 36 (1978): 405–17.
3. S. Berglas, "Self-handicapping and Self-handicappers: A Cognitive/ Attributional Model of Interpersonal Self-protective Behavior," in *Perspectives in Personality*, vol. 1, ed. R. Hogan and W. H. Jones (Greenwich, Conn.: JAI Press, 1985), pp. 235–70. See also M. R. Leary and J. A. Shepperd, "Behavioral Self-handicaps versus Self-reported Handicaps: A Conceptual Note," *Journal of Personality and Social Psychology* 51 (1986): 1265–68.
4. C. R. Snyder, "Excuses," *Psychology Today*, pp. 50–55. See also R. L. Higgins and S. Berglas, "The Maintenance and Treatment of Self-handicapping: From Risk-taking to Face-saving—and Back," in *Self-handicapping*, Higgins, Snyder, and Berglas, pp. 198–200.
5. S. Berglas, "A Typology of Self-handicapping Alcohol Abusers," in *Advances in Applied Social Psychology*, vol. 3, ed. M. J. Saks and L. Saxe (Hillsdale, N.J.: Erlbaum, 1986), pp. 29–56.
6. D. M. Tice and R. F. Baumeister, "Self-esteem, Self-handicapping, and Self-presentation: The Strategy of Inadequate Practice," *Journal of Personality* 58 (1990): 443–64.
7. R. J. Gelles, *The Violent Home* (Beverly Hills, Calif.: Sage, 1972), p. 116.
8. C. H. McCaghy, "Drinking and Deviance Disavowal: The Case of Child Molesters," *Social Problems* 16 (1968): 43–49.
9. Ibid., p. 48.
10. B. Critchlow, "The Blame in the Bottle: Attributions about Drunken Behavior," *Personality and Social Psychology Bulletin* 11 (1985): 258–74.
11. P. G. W. Schouten and M. M. Handelsman, "Social Basis of Self-handicapping: The Case of Depression," *Personality and Social Psychology Bulletin* 13 (1987): 103–10.
12. S. Waldman, "Tippling in Washington: How Traditions Change," *Newsweek*, March 6, 1989, p. 23.
13. For a discussion of the role that generic uncertainty plays in precipitating self-handicapping, see Higgins, Snyder, and Berglas, *Self-handicapping*, pp. 110–12.

14. J. Durso, "The Sudden Fall of a Baseball Phenomenon," *New York Times,* Apr. 5, 1987, p. 1.

15. See S. Berglas, "Self-handicapping Alcohol Abusers"; and S. Berglas, "Self-handicapping and Psychopathology: An Integration of Social and Clinical Perspectives," in *Social Processes in Clinical and Consulting Psychology,* ed. J. E. Maddux, C. D. Stoltenberg, and R. Rosenwein (New York: Springer-Verlag, 1987), pp. 113–25.

16. For further discussion of what constituted noncontingent success, see L. Y. Abramson, M. E. P. Seligman, and J. D. Teasdale, "Learned Helplessness in Humans: Critique and Reformulation," *Journal of Abnormal Psychology* 87 (1978): 49–74.

17. See S. Berglas and E. E. Jones, "Drug Choice as a Self-handicapping Strategy in Response to Noncontingent Success," *Journal of Personality and Social Psychology* 36 (1978): 405–17; and E. E. Jones and S. Berglas, "Control of Attributions about the Self through Self-handicapping Strategies: The Appeal of Alcohol and the Role of Underachievement," *Personality and Social Psychiatry Bulletin,* 4 (1978): 200–206.

18. Berglas, "Self-handicapping and Psychopathology."

19. "Adventure. Lost Love, New Films: At Twenty-nine Candy Bergen Is Growing Up," *People,* July 28, 1975, p. 48.

20. E. Jacobson, "The 'Exceptions': An Elaboration of Freud's Character Study," *Psychoanalytic Study of the Child* 14 (1959): 135–54.

21. Berglas, "Self-handicapping and Psychopathology."

22. S. Duval and R. A. Wicklund, *A Theory of Objective Self-awareness* (New York: Academic Press, 1972).

23. J. G. Hull and R. D. Young, "Self-consciousness, Self-esteem, and Success–failure as Determinants of Alcohol Consumption in Male Social Drinkers," *Journal of Personality and Social Psychology* 44 (1983): 1097–1109.

24. See, for example, R. Radloff, "Social Comparison and Ability Evaluation," *Journal of Experimental Social Psychology,* supp. (1966): 6–26.

25. A. Bandura, "Self-efficacy: Toward a Unifying Theory of Behavioral Change," *Psychological Review* 84 (1977): 191–215.

26. S. Berglas, *The Success Syndrome: Hitting Bottom When You Reach the Top* (New York: Plenum, 1986), pp. 144–45, 155–56.

27. S. Berglas, "Self-handicapping: Etiological and Diagnostic Considerations," in *Self-handicapping,* R. L. Higgins, C. R. Snyder, and S. Berglas, pp. 151–86. See also Berglas and Jones, "Drug Choice as a Self-handicapping Strategy," p. 406.

28. E. Berne, *Games People Play: The Psychology of Human Relationships* (New York: Castle Books, 1964).

29. See, for example, D. W. Tressmer, *Fear of Success* (New York: Plenum, 1977); and J. O. Cavenar and D. S. Werman, "Origins of the Fear of Success," *American Journal of Psychiatry* 138 (1981): 95–98.

30. S. Freud, "Some Character Types Met in Psychoanalytic Work," in *Collected Papers,* vol. 4 (New York: Basic Books, 1949), pp. 318–44; original work published in 1915.

31. H. S. Sullivan, *The Interpersonal Theory of Psychiatry* (New York: Norton, 1953).

32. For an explanation of how self-handicapping can augment ability attributions, see S. Berglas, "Self-handicapping and Self-handicappers: A Cognitive/Attributional Model of Interpersonal Self-protective Behavior," in *Perspectives in Personality,* vol. 1, ed. R. Hogan and W. H. Jones (Greenwich, Conn.: JAI Press, 1985), pp. 235–70; and H. H. Kelley, *Attribution in Social Interaction* (Morristown, N.J.: General Learning Press, 1971).

33. D. M. Tice, "Esteem Protection of Enhancement? Self-handicapping Motives and Attributions" *Journal of Personality and Social Psychology* 60 (1991): 711–25.

34. See, for example, H. Selye, *The Stress of Life* (New York: McGraw-Hill, 1976); and R. S. Lazarus and R. Launier, "Stress Related Transactions between Person and Environment," in *Perspectives in Interactional Psychology,* ed. L. A. Pervin and M. Lewis (New York: Plenum, 1978), pp. 287–327.

35. W. James, *Principles of Psychology,* vol. 1 (London: Macmillan, 1901), p. 310.

36. See, for example, T. W. Smith, C. R. Snyder, and M. M. Handelsman, "On the Self-serving Function of an Academic Wooden Leg: Text Anxiety as a Self-handicapping Strategy," *Journal of Personality and Social Psychology* 42 (1982): 314–21.

37. D. Ansen, "Greta Garbo: 1905–1990," *Newsweek,* Apr. 30, 1990, p. 73; emphasis added.

38. C. R. Snyder, T. W. Smith, and R. E. Ingram, "On the Self-serving Function of Anxiety. Shyness as a Self-handicapping strategy," *Journal of Personality and Social Psychology* 48 (1985): 970–80. See also P. Zimbardo, *Shyness* (Reading, Mass.: Addison-Wesley, 1977), for a discussion of shyness as a psychological disorder.

39. C. R. Snyder, T. W. Smith, R. W. Augelli, and R. E. Ingram, "On the

Self-serving Function of Social Anxiety," *Journal of Personality and Social Psychology* 48 (1985): 970–80.

Chapter 6:
Pyrrhic Revenge

1. For a review of the literature related to this self-defeating style, see S. Berglas, "Self-handicapping Behavior and the Self-defeating Personality Disorder: Toward a Refined Clinical Perspective," in *Self-defeating Behaviors: Experimental Research, Clinical Impressions, and Practical Implications,* ed. R. C. Curtis (New York: Plenum, 1989), pp. 266–68.
2. American Psychiatric Association, *Diagnostic and Statistical Manual of Mental Disorders,* 3rd ed., rev. (Washington, D.C.: Author, 1987), p. 325.
3. See, for example, B. Berliner, "The Role of Object Relations in Moral Masochism," *Psychoanalytic Quarterly* 27 (1958): 38–56.
4. W. Reich, *Character Analysis* (New York: Orgone Institute Press, 1933).
5. R. D. Stolorow, "The Narcissistic Function of Masochism (and Sadism)," *International Journal of Psychoanalysis* 56 (1975): 441–48.
6. For a review of this observation, see R. L. Sack and W. Miller, "Masochism: A Clinical and Theoretical Overview," *Psychiatry* 38 (1975): 244–57; and Berglas, "Self-handicapping Behavior," p. 267.
7. J. Aronfreed, "Aversive Control of Socialization," in *Nebraska Symposium on Motivation,* vol. 16 (Lincoln: University of Nebraska Press, 1968).
8. See, for example, N. L. Corah and J. Boffa, "Perceived Control, Self-observation, and Response to Aversive Stimuli," *Journal of Personality and Social Psychology* 16 (1970): 1–4.
9. B. F. Skinner, *Science and Human Behavior* (New York: Free Press, 1953), p. 367.
10. American Psychiatric Association, *Diagnostic and Statistical Manual,* p. 55.
11. S. Brody, "Syndrome of the Treatment-Rejecting Patient," *Psychoanalytic Review* 51 (1964): 75–84; E. Berne, *Games People Play: The Psychology of Human Relationships* (New York: Castle Books, 1964).
12. T. Reik, *Masochism in Modern Man* (New York: Farrar and Strauss, 1941).
13. Stolorow, "Narcissistic Function."
14. For a more detailed discussion of this dynamic, see Berglas, "Self-handicapping Behavior," pp. 267–68.
15. See Reik, *Masochism.*

16. Ibid.

17. For a more detailed discussion of masochism, see R. F. Baumeister, "Masochism as Escape from Self," *Journal of Sex Research* 25 (1988): 28–59; and R. F. Baumeister, *Masochism and the Self* (Hillsdale, N.J.: Erlbaum, 1989).

18. B. van der Kolk, "The Compulsion to Repeat the Trauma: Reenactment, Revictimization, and Masochism," *Treatment of Victims of Sexual Abuse* 12 (1989): 389–411.

19. See, for example, R. L. Solomon, "An Opponent-Process Theory of Acquired Motivation: The Costs of Pleasure and the Benefits of Pain," *American Psychologist* 35 (1980): 691–712; and G. M. Erschak, "The Escalation and Maintenance of Spouse Abuse: A Cybernetic Model," *Victimology* 9 (1984): 247–53.

20. M. H. Silbert and A. M. Pines, "Sexual Child Abuse as an Antecedent to Prostitution," *Child Abuse and Negligence* 5 (1981): 407–11.

Chapter 7:
Resolving the Tragic Paradox

1. For a preliminary discussion of this issue, see S. Berglas, "Self-handicapping Behavior and the Self-defeating Personality Disorder: Toward a Refined Clinical Perspective," in *Self-defeating Behaviors: Experimental Research, Clinical Impressions, and Practical Implications,* ed. R. C. Curtis (New York: Plenum, 1989).

2. Drs. Susan Fiester and John Gunderson, research meeting with Dr. Steven Berglas, McLean Hospital, Belmont, Mass., October 5, 1990.

3. C. Lasch, *The Culture of Narcissism* (New York: Norton, 1978).

4. S. E. Taylor, *Positive Illusions: Creative Self-deception and the Healthy Mind* (New York: Basic Books, 1981); S. E. Taylor and J. D. Brown, "Illusion and Well-being: A Social Psychological Perspective on Mental Health," *Psychological Bulletin* 103 (1988): 193–210.

5. See D. Kahneman, P. Slovic, and A. Tversky, *Judgment under Uncertainty: Heuristics and Biases* (Cambridge: Cambridge University Press, 1982).

6. S. Berglas, *The Success Syndrome* (New York: Plenum, 1986).

7. A. M. Isen, T. E. Nygren, and F. G. Ashby, "Influence of Positive Affect on the Subjective Utility of Gains and Losses: It Is Just Not Worth the Risk," *Journal of Personality and Social Psychology* 55 (1988): 710–17.

8. R. F. Baumeister and A. M. Stillwell, "Negative Affect and Self-defeating Choices" (Unpublished research data, Case Western Reserve University, 1992).

9. D. M. Tice, "Esteem Protection or Enhancement? Self-handicapping Motives and Attributions Differ by Trait Self-esteem," *Journal of Personality and Social Psychology* 60 (1991): 711–25.

10. R. F. Baumeister, ed., *Public Self and Private Self* (New York: Springer, 1986); B. R. Schlenker, *Impression Management: The Self-concept, Social Identity, and Interpersonal Relations* (Monterey, Calif.: Brooks/Cole, 1980).

11. T. A. Kolditz and R. M. Arkin, "An Impression Management Interpretation of the Self-handicapping Strategy," *Journal of Personality and Social Psychology* 43 (1982): 492–502; D. M. Tice and R. F. Baumeister, "Self-esteem, Self-handicapping, and Self-presentation: The Strategy of Inadequate Practice," *Journal of Personality* 58 (1990): 443–64.

12. R. F. Baumeister, J. C. Hamilton, and D. M. Tice, "Public versus Private Expectancy of Success: Confidence Booster or Performance Pressure?" *Journal of Personality and Social Psychology* 48 (1985): 1447–57; B. R. Schlenker and M. R. Leary, "Social Anxiety and Self-presentation: A Conceptualization and Model," *Psychological Bulletin* 92 (1982): 641–69; F. V. Fox and B. M. Staw, "The Trapped Administrator: Effects of Insecurity and Policy Resistance upon Commitment to a Course of Action," *Administrative Sciences Quarterly* 24 (1979): 449–71.

13. R. L. Higgins and S. Berglas, "The Maintenance and Treatment of Self-handicapping: From Risk-taking to Face-saving—and Back," in *Self-handicapping: The Paradox That Isn't,* R. L. Higgins, C. R. Snyder, and S. Berglas (New York: Plenum), pp. 187–238.

14. S. Freud, *Civilization and Its Discontents* (New York: Norton, 1930).

Index